A Time of Renewal

A TIME OF RENEWAL

Daily Reflections for the Lenten Season

by

MOTHER MARY FRANCIS, P.C.C.

IGNATIUS PRESS SAN FRANCISCO

Cover art:
Christ Bearing the Cross
Andrea Solario (1460–1524)
RestoredTraditions.com

Cover design by Riz Boncan Marsella

Interior illustrations by
Sister Mary Pius, P.C.C.
Newport News, Virginia

ISBN 978-1-58617-977-9
Library of Congress Control Number 2014944004
Printed in the United States of America ♾

In gratitude
to Mother Mary Francis,
our beloved abbess and mother for forty-one years,
who taught us how to make the angels dance

CONTENTS

FIRST WEEK OF LENT

SECOND WEEK OF LENT

THIRD WEEK OF LENT

FOURTH WEEK OF LENT

FIFTH WEEK OF LENT

HOLY WEEK

FOREWORD

Eight centuries ago, a ragged band of barefoot vagabonds set out across Europe seeking literally to live the Gospel as Jesus did, and captivated the world-weary medieval mind and imagination. Long before they were called "Franciscans" they were known as "mendicant friars", *Fratres minores*, and *joculares*. Perhaps the most intriguing title applied to these men was "the joyful penitents from Assisi". This description captures perfectly the spirit in which the Franciscans view penance. It is not a glum, gloomy, drab affair, but a glorious and great privilege leading to true joy. In his biography of Saint Francis, G.K. Chesterton observed:

> The whole point about Saint Francis of Assisi is that he certainly was ascetical and he certainly was not gloomy. As soon as ever he had been unhorsed by the glorious humiliation of his vision of dependence on the divine love, he flung himself into fasting and vigil exactly as he had flung himself furiously into battle. He had wheeled his charger clean round, but there was no halt or check in the thundering impetuosity of his charge. There was nothing negative about it; . . . it was as positive as a passion; it had all the air of being as positive as a pleasure. He devoured fasting as a man devours food. He plunged after poverty as men have dug madly for gold.[1]

[1] G.K. Chesterton, *Saint Thomas Aquinas and Saint Francis of Assisi* (San Francisco: Ignatius Press, 1986), 77–78.

As a faithful daughter of Saints Francis and Clare, Mother Mary Francis is thoroughly imbued with their spirit. Readers of her writings have already encountered her Franciscan approach to ongoing conversion as she ponders this paradox:

> This is what is so deeply in my heart, which I want you to take deeply into your own heart, your own reflection, your own prayer. When we are not alert to make reparation for our sins and our faults, it is because we do not have a prayerful awareness of them. We simply see a situation that calls for effort that we do not want to make, that calls for generosity we are not prepared to give, that calls for us to humble ourselves in a way we do not wish. But the penitent sees something so different—and the penitent is joyful. The real penitent is always ready to go, full of purpose, full of alertness, full of Joy. Like Saint Francis, we are all called to be joyful penitents.[2]

In the present collection of reflections, Mother makes penance and conversion both attractive and desirable, and Lent viewed through the lucid lens of her Poor Clare perception becomes an opportunity to be embraced rather than an obstacle to be endured or avoided.

And so, from the "Poor Lady" who penned *A Right to Be Merry*, we find the wisdom of a woman with the delightful audacity to suggest that joy is not out of place in the season of penance, but is essential to understanding the true nature of the season. She encourages us to wel-

[2] From *Come, Lord Jesus: Meditations on the Art of Waiting* (San Francisco: Ignatius Press, 2010), 138.

come Lent with open arms as God's personal invitation to enter into joy: "We are called to a glorious festival of love—to be spiritually dizzied with the fact that this is how much God has loved us. Surely we shall all look at the crucifix with a new vision, a deepened understanding that he really did this, he loved us this much."

Father John Riley
Augustine Institute
Greenwood Village, Colorado

INTRODUCTION

Years ago, we were privileged to welcome two young novices from one of our Poor Clare monasteries in Japan to spend time in a larger novitiate group for their religious formation. Mother Mary Francis was explaining to them during her instructions that truthful acknowledgment of our faults is a prerequisite for prayer. Since their English was not fluent, she resorted to gestures to illustrate her words. Commenting on the passage from Luke 15 that there is joy among the angels in heaven upon one sinner doing penance, she struck her breast and flapped her arms to demonstrate a rejoicing angel. The Japanese novices giggled in delight, and the point was well made. Later Mother wrote this poem:

Choreography for Angels[1]

"I say to you, that there is joy among the angels in heaven upon one sinner doing penance . . ." (Luke 15:10)

Who spun these Angels into dance
When wars are needing all artillery
Of spirits' cannonading. Armistice
Wants first the over-powering wings, and they
Are occupied with pirouettes! Who did this?

Gone penitent, I caused it. I confess it.

[1] First published in Mother Mary Francis, *Summon Spirit's Cry: A Collection of Poems* (San Francisco: Ignatius Press, 1996), 37–38.

Who tilted flames of Seraphim
In arabesques of pure delightedness?
Is not the cosmic crisis begging fire
For full destruction of hate's hazarding!
Why Seraphs swirling flames on floors of heaven?

I lit the heavens, when I bent my head.

Who lined mystic *corps-de-ballet*
Of Cherubim? Who set in pas-de-deux
This Power with this Principality?
Why these Archangels not on mission sent
Today, but waltzing on the stars, and singing?

I am the one who did this. I confess it.
I smote my errant heart, and Angels danced.

This is but one example of how Mother Mary Francis adroitly persuaded her spiritual daughters to regard penance as a joyful enterprise. Year after year, she tirelessly poured out all the resources of her great heart and intellect to instruct us in the art of prayer, which begins with truthful self-confrontation. Her chapter conferences span a period of forty-one years and examine every facet of the spiritual life in an engaging and accessible way.

Responding to the suggestion of readers who have appreciated Mother's conferences for the season of Advent in *Come, Lord Jesus: Meditations on the Art of Waiting*, we have prepared a similar volume for Lent. Some of the conferences are a commentary on the actual texts given for the readings of the day; others have been selected to complement the theme of the day's readings.

"Lent" is a Middle English word that means "spring", expressing the anticipated outcome of this penitential season. We hope these reflections will cultivate a splendid spiritual springtime in those who read them.

The Poor Clare Nuns
Monastery of Our Lady of Guadalupe
Roswell, New Mexico

A Time of Reflowering

We have come to the beginning of Lent, and I hope we will not allow ourselves to think of it as "just another Lent". There is a very deep sense in which there is not another Lent and then another and another after that. This Lent is unlike any other. It is *this* acceptable time. We do not know if there will be another Lent for us, but we do know God has brought us to this acceptable time, to this prolonged day of salvation. This is the acceptable time, and the Apostle Paul is begging us not to receive the graces of this time in vain (see 2 Cor 6:1). He is also implying that there will be struggle, that this is a great testing ground, and that as we grow in our awareness of our need for redemption and in a very humble attitude toward others, so do we nourish the will to make a sustained effort to do better. By all of these things we enter into the mystery of our communal life in the Church. We are responsible for one another's holiness. We influence each other all the time, and we should grow in the awareness of this. It simply cannot be denied that we are conditioned and affected by one another. Human beings invariably are. Every Christian has a vocation to holiness.

Now as we enter into Lent, I hope we will all be deeply conscious of our involvement in one another's holiness, of our sharing of penance and of sacrifice, and very especially of our responsibility for one another's growth in holiness this Lent.

Our Lord tells us in today's Gospel to keep secrets with him: "When you give alms, do not let your left hand know what your right hand is doing, so that your alms may be in secret; and your Father who sees in secret will reward you" (Mt 6:3–4). What does that have to do with our spiritual lives? We have to smile ruefully and say, "Quite a bit." Is it not true, to our miserable shame, that sometimes we say we will do something for another, but it will be made clear that this is costing us a great deal? "Oh, yes. I will give this service, I will give this time, I will rise to the occasion, but I hope it is clear to everyone that this is not easy." We want to keep the secrets of the Lord when giving alms.

The Gospel on Sunday will tell us that our Lord was led into the desert to be tempted. He entered into this period, which we now call Lent, to suffer. There was a specific purpose: he went to be tempted. There is a great mystery in those words. When we enter into Lent, we should be aware that we will be tempted. Let us pray not to be found wanting, pray very humbly that the grace of God in us shall not be in vain. The Apostle says, "We entreat you not to accept the grace of God in vain" (2 Cor 6:1). Holy Mother Church is a loving Mother, and she says in the hymn for Lent, the "Audi, Benigne Conditor", "O God, you know how feeble our strength is." She tells us how to pray. Let us pray to him this way: "Here we come enthusiastically, bravely out into the desert to be tempted but, dear Lord, don't forget. You know how feeble our strength is and that we don't want to receive the grace of God in vain." We walk out bravely, enthusiastically on shaky little legs.

The beautiful hymn at Lauds, "Iam, Christe, Sol Justitiae", says, "*Dies venit, dies tua, in qua reflorent omnia.*" "The day comes, your day, in which everything comes to flower again." Lent is meant to bring us to a reflowering, and as Lent is beginning, let us have the purpose of Lent in mind: that everything may flower again. Our Lord has told us again and again that there is no life without death. There is no beauty without a digging of the ground so that it might come forth. Let us look toward the end of Lent, so that the suffering has a meaning. We know we do these penitential things for a purpose, and that if we do them well, if we try with our feeble strength, depending on the divine strength, not to let his grace be in vain, then this Lent should be for us the time in which everything flowers again. We see things heaving up through the earth, destroying the drabness and dreariness of winter. We see everything beginning to flower again, the latent beauty that is always slumbering in nature quite literally breaking forth. We have this image of what our Lenten observance should be. All the world around us is becoming more beautiful in its *reflorilegium*.

Saint Francis loved to look at the image of God in all of

creation. He prayed, "Who are you and who am I?" What struck him was not, "How nothing am I", but, "How great am I". He never depreciated himself, although he often depreciated and bewailed and bemoaned his behavior. He saw that he often failed to flower again, to come up to God's expectations of him. This is what drew cries from the heart of Francis. He said, "If the greatest sinner in the world had been given the grace and light I have been given, he would have been greater and holier than I." He was saying this because it was true. This was a man who recognized the truth and knew to what great things he was called. We, too, are called to great things in this Lenten springtime.

Thursday after Ash Wednesday

❧

Choose Life

Today's First Reading speaks of the power we have to choose what is right: "I have set before you life and death, the blessing and the curse. Choose life, then, that you and your descendants may live, by loving the Lord, your God, heeding his voice, and holding fast to him. For that will mean life for you" (Dt 30:19–20, NAB). We know that the Israelites often failed to keep the commandments. Without his saving grace it was not possible for fallen human nature to keep the commandments, much less to rise to the heights of holiness. This is what the Redeemer has made possible for us. He has set us free; he has delivered us from the powers of darkness.

The book of Sirach says, "To act faithfully is a matter of your own choice" (Sir 15:15). How shall I respond to that? Well, I want to be faithful. I start out in the morning: I'm going to be so faithful. I am full of this resolve, and God knows that I am sincere. I want this to be the perfect Lent, and I want to be utterly faithful. Then I find I've been unfaithful to grace. What do I do then? We go back to the Lenten liturgy, which tells us that Lent is for sinners, Lent is for the miserable, Lent is for the wretched. This says it all. The Church is telling us in Lent that we're the ones it's all about. If you're not a sinner, then step out of line, because all these Lenten graces aren't for you. But it is the one who falls and rises who understands the need for Lent. This is the heroism: not that we never fall, but that we keep on rising.

To behave faithfully is a matter of our own choice. So we can be very faithful in our contrition. We can be very faithful in our humility. We can be very faithful in admitting that we were wrong. We can be very faithful in saying, "I could have done much better." We can be very faithful in laughing at ourselves. In this sense (I say it with all gravity), Lent should be a season for laughter. Doesn't this seem strange for a season of penance? Well, no. Lent is a season for directing laughter toward ourselves. Not sardonic laughter, not cynical laughter ("Who, you? You think you're going to be a saint? Do you think you can achieve the heights?"), but the gentle laughter that says, "O God, be merciful to me, a sinner." That kind of divine humor about our own weakness helps us to understand what the Lenten liturgy is about. When we are so wholeheartedly contrite, God tells us, "I don't even remember that it happened."

If we want to behave faithfully, it is in our power. Let us remember that to be faithful includes being faithfully contrite, being faithfully humble, being faithfully realistic, being faithfully true. We have no reason to be downhearted in Lent. We have no reason to be downhearted when we fail. If our aspirations are high and we sometimes do not reach them, then we try harder and we are faithfully contrite.

Yesterday, the prophet Joel told us that Lent is the season for sinners, those poor little people trying to do better. By the words that the inspired prophet uses, we should be raised to heights of enthusiasm for God's forgiveness and for our efforts for holiness. Joel expresses God's tender invitation, "Return to me with . . . fasting and weeping and mourning" (Joel 2:12, NAB). He doesn't say, "Now begin fasting and mourning", but "Return to me." God takes it for granted that we have not been perfect, that we have not been paragons of holiness. When we are conscious of our sins and our faults, that is when God is calling to us. The prophet says again, "Return to God with your whole heart." Wholehearted contrition is a very great thing, and fills us with happiness.

What kind of choices are we going to make? He has delivered us, but we can choose to descend to the darkness. He has brought us over into the kingdom of light, but we can choose to go back into the shadows. He is saying, "Return to me." We can choose to say, "No, thank you. I don't like fasting, weeping, and mourning. I prefer my mediocrity."

We can choose to be unredeemed. We are delivered from the powers of darkness, but we are perfectly free to go back (see Col 1:13). We are brought into the kingdom of light, but we can choose to stray out of the kingdom. This is the great choice of Lent: to behave faithfully is in our power. Fire and water are set before man. We can choose whatever we please: fire that burns our hands and our souls, or the water of grace that always refreshes us. God is very merciful toward our failings. God cannot help us when we choose to be mediocre, when we choose to be burned and to stay burned.

The redemption is accomplished and yet always continues until the end of time by each right choice we make. This is our Lenten power—to make our choices wholeheartedly every day, in little practical ways and with a great sense of poverty and responsibility before the Lord. When we see we have made poor choices, then let us behave faithfully by our contrition.

Friday after Ash Wednesday

God's Lenten Program

God lays out for us in the First Reading today a very stern and glorious program through the prophet Isaiah: "Your fast ends in quarreling and fighting, striking with wicked claw" (Is 58:4, NAB). These are chilling things to reflect upon, and they should be. Certainly God wants us to deepen our prayer. He is telling us these are the things that will come if we are really persons of prayer: "This, rather, is the fasting that I wish: releasing those bound unjustly, untying the thongs of the yoke; setting free the oppressed, breaking every yoke; sharing your bread with the hungry, sheltering the oppressed and the homeless; clothing the naked when you see them, and not turning your back on your own" (Is 58:6–7, NAB). If these are not the things we are concerned with, then God is saying that he would put a big question mark on our prayer.

There are eight points in God's Lenten program, all leading to fraternal love. We release those who are bound unjustly. We untie the thongs. We set the oppressed free. We break every yoke. We share our bread. We shelter the homeless. We clothe the naked. We do not turn our back on anyone. Now all of those eight points, like the spiritual and corporal works of mercy, have tremendous meaning for us. Let us be quite shaken by this understanding of what God calls Lent: that charity is showing itself in all these ways; and if it is not, then Lent is not a success in his eyes.

We can only go forward rightly by following God's lead. What does it mean to release those who are bound unjustly? It means to stop blaming other people for our own lack of growth. To blame our own faults on others is to bind them unjustly. This is one of the greatest delusions in the world: that I would be so patient if, if, if. I would be so charitable if, if, if. The truth is not that I am impatient because of so-and-so interrupting me or frustrating me or wasting my time. Rather, that person reveals to me my own lack. She reveals to me the shallowness of my prayer, the flimsiness of my charity, the superficiality of my patience. The right response is to blame myself.

The second point is to untie the thongs. What does that mean for us? I think it has great meaning in every situation where human beings live together. Things will always be getting, as we say colloquially, tied up, jammed up. We are to resolve these things, not to say, "Why is this? Why are there ripples on the water?" There are a lot of ripples on the water, but we can always smooth, always make things better. Resolve the situation. Untie it. Smooth the waters. Pour oil upon troubled waters. This is what we are supposed to be doing, not marveling that situations do get into little knots. Of course they will, wherever there are human beings. But this is what Lent is: I am always doing what I can to make it better. That comes through practice, with God's grace. If only that could come to be our first response all the time: What can I do to make it better? We will always know, if we put that question to ourselves.

Then the third point is to set the oppressed free. Well, who is oppressed? Are there any captives around here? Yes, we are all captives in some way to our weaknesses, our limitations, our dullness, our obtuseness, our lack of understanding, our faults, our sins. How do we help these struggling captives? We do this in a very ordinary way: by smiling at one another, by bringing joy to one another. God says, "Set the oppressed free." Oppression of its very definition is heaviness; we are weighed down. We relieve oppression by our sweetness, by our smiles. Remember the continual reply of Mother Teresa of Calcutta to those who asked her, "What shall we do?" She said, "Smile at each other." This is how we relieve one another's oppression. We know we are weighed down by someone who looks scowling, dark, or withdrawn, and we know how much is changed by a person's smile, a joyful face. We are set free, we feel lighter. That is how I set the oppressed free: by letting another know by my face that she is loved. When we are aware that we are loved, then what oppressions remain weigh very lightly.

God's fourth point is to break every yoke. Now again, each one of us has her own unique yoke. I am not speaking of the yoke of Jesus, which he says is sweet and light; but our own yoke, the yoke of our personal misery. We have the yoke and the burden of ourselves to bear: the high ideal, and yet the poor expression of it often enough. We are to break those yokes in one another. It is only love that understands. If we do not love and are not always expanding that love, then instead of growing in the realization of our own misery, we will become more and more demanding with the wrong questions, "Why does she do that? Why is it this way?" Then we judge, "This should stop." We make the yoke heavier. We must never forget that another's faults do weigh upon her. If we are occupied with thinking how they weigh upon us, we are apt to forget that. Yet when we each look into ourselves, we know that none of us is happy with her own faults. We know our faults are a weight upon us. They are a yoke upon us. The more we are breaking the yokes of others by being understanding of them, then the more we are able, with God's grace, to break free of our own yoke.

The fifth point is to share our bread with the hungry. That is quite obvious, isn't it? God is saying we should be much more generous. What bread do we have to share? We have the bread of our time. We have the bread of our interest in those who want us to show interest in what is of interest to them. We have the bread of multiple ways of showing concern: always sharing our bread, always being concerned, always being interested, always having the time for the little extra touch that means so much.

As I was reflecting on that, a little story we read years ago came flying into my mind. One of Pope Saint John XXIII's high-placed visitors had left behind a very heavy sweater, a very fine one. You can understand that, if you were with the Holy Father, you wouldn't remember much of anything except that you were with the Holy Father. The Pope himself pinned a little note on the sweater which read, "I really don't need this, so I'm sending it back to you." The Pope took a few seconds to write that note himself and put it on the sweater. I'm sure that cardinal probably framed it. He probably looked at it every day. It was what might be called such a little thing. He shared his time with the hungry; he shared his bread with the hungry. We can, too, in multiple ways.

The sixth point is to shelter the homeless. In our immediate surroundings, we may not have anyone who is physically homeless. But when we feel we are not understood, there is a sense in which we are homeless. And so we must always provide a home of understanding. There will inevitably be times when we do not understand someone's behavior or a certain response, but we can understand the person. Although we may sometimes wish she would do differently, we can understand that under the blunders (and we all have our share of them), there is someone who wants to do the right thing.

God's seventh point is to clothe the naked. This is similar to making things right. It is always smoothing over; it is always forgiving. We are all stripped before one another. If we try to be pretentious, if we try to be artificial, if we try to camouflage, we make ourselves ridiculous. We are on display to one another. We are very poor, and in that way unclothed before one another. We must always be clothing one another with forgiveness, with love, always ransoming this stripped captive back again, always.

The final point is not turning our back on anyone. This, of course, we do by our awareness of one another, by listening to one another. One hunches one's shoulders in dismay to say it, but it's true—we choose not to turn our back by refusing to be bored with one another, because God is never bored with us. I think any of us would be honest enough to say, "I'm sure that I am very boring in the little interior recordings I keep playing, the little excuses I keep making, the drabness and the dreariness of my responses." But God never succumbs to boredom with us. He is always interested; he is always aware.

Let us fulfill God's Lenten program, and not delude ourselves that there is any other program to compare with his.

Saturday after Ash Wednesday

The Divine Physician

As we enter into Lent, let us explore the question: What is a penitent? How does one become a penitent? It seems to me there are three ideas that emerge.

The first one of these three is an awareness of sin. Obviously one cannot be a penitent unless one thinks she has some reason for doing penance. I think if there is a particular lacuna in the philosophy of our times, if I may use such an over-simplification, it is the loss of the consciousness of sin. We are so occupied with trying to break down people's guilt complexes, in trying to establish healthy mental outlooks, that we may have gotten a little confused about the very great difference there is between a guilt complex and a sense of guilt. Certainly a guilt complex is a very bad thing. It avails nothing. It hinders us on the path to holiness, to God. But on the other hand, a consciousness of guilt is essential to becoming holy, to growing in love.

What we want to recover at the beginning of Lent, if we have lost it in any measure, is a consciousness of our culpability, a very deep and unperturbed sense of our need of redemption. How can we know if we have lost it? A very sure gauge of this is how hard we are on other people, how much we complain about other people, how alert we are for the faults of other people. If we have lost a sense of our own guiltiness, our own need of redemption, then the energy that should be applied in correcting what this consciousness reveals will have to be turned in another direction and inevitably, it will turn to the faults of others. It will become very corrective toward others. It will see many faults in others. So let us use this little gauge to discover how deep our consciousness of our own guilt is.

We are foolish if we do not grow and abide in this consciousness of our own faultiness, since we are cutting ourselves off from the group of persons for whom the Son of God particularly came. What does he tell us in the Scriptures? He says it is the sick who need a physician. So if we think that other people are obviously ailing, that there is not too much wrong with us, then this is a way of saying to our dear Lord, "Pass on. I don't need you. You were not sent for me." This is a terrible thought, is it not? Yet Eternal Truth said that he came for sick people; he came for people who are ailing; he came to heal people who are not well. The first thing a person has to do is to call on the Physician, and admit he is sick and needs help. "I have not come to call the righteous, but sinners to repentance" (Lk 5:32). Well, we want to be called. But it is only when we acknowledge our faultiness, our sinfulness, when we are glad and grateful to be corrected, to be helped to become less sinful, that we are numbering ourselves among those to whom he specifically was sent.

Then he says through his precursor, "Bear fruits that befit repentance" (Lk 3:8). There are no two ways about it. This was not a welcome message in Saint John the Baptist's time, it wasn't in Jeremiah's time, and, very particularly, it is not today. It seems a large part of the world is bemused with the idea that all we need to do is wander through creation, admiring it, having a great spirit of camaraderie with our fellows, and everything will be fine. No cross is needed anymore. We needn't give any attention to penance. We have outgrown this now. We have discovered that this is a great health-giving, self-sanctifying world, and all we need to do is to be utterly involved in it, and everything shall turn out beautifully. The trouble with this philosophy is that it doesn't work. It never has worked. The Son of God pointed this out himself, his precursor pointed this out, and his Church is still pointing it out.

The effect of this awareness of our guilt is not agitation, but a great peace. This might seem like a paradox, and it is; but the whole spiritual life is built on paradox. We have all surely experienced that the moment in which we admit our faults and are truly conscious of them, is at the same time our moment of greatest peace. It is at such times that we are filled with a great sense of wonder that we should have been wanted by God, that we should be tolerated by other people. It is out of such sentiments that real humility springs, that real peace is begotten and nourished. On the other hand, a lack of consciousness of our own sinfulness and guilt only begets agitation.

The second essential quality of a penitent is a desire to change direction. That is the real meaning of the Greek word *metanoia*, which means "a reversal, a change of direction". After the awareness that we are deficient, we have to desire to do something about this. We can't just say, "Well, that's true, that's the way I am", and then, as it were, sit down with this idea. But we have to stand on our two spiritual feet and with God's grace turn ourselves around, reverse our direction; and to carry this desire into practice we need enthusiasm. If we are not enthusiastic about changing our direction, we shall never do it. We shall simply be theoreticians. We need the high enthusiasm of Saint Francis of Assisi and Saint Clare. Neither of them ever did anything halfway. They were extremely enthusiastic people. That's why they could surprise the world with astonishing statements such as "merry penitents" and "being joyous in the penitential life". They discovered their own deficiencies; they determined to reverse their directions, and they did it with a sense of high enthusiasm.

The third quality of a penitent is energetic determination of will. Awareness of our faults avails us nothing if it does not beget in us an enthusiasm to change. Enthusiasm without a sustained effort quickly peters out. Awareness and enthusiasm must be fulfilled in an energetic will to overcome our faults and sins.

When we call out to the Divine Physician, he will answer, "Here I am" if we call as sinners and not as "the righteous ones". We want to grow in spiritual stature, and in order to help us do this he has to give us some bitter remedies to take. We do not purge poisons out of the system without taking bitter medicine. He has to perform some therapy on us that is very painful. We do not get dislocated joints back into place without pain.

Let us rehearse those three points in our minds; they are very simple. They are easy to remember—nothing sensational, nothing original—but I do think they are vital points in life. Let us go into this Lent with a sense of enthusiasm, a deep consciousness of sin, an awareness that we are penitents in need of redemption, and a knowledge that we are ailing people whom the Physician is coming to heal.

FIRST WEEK OF LENT

First Sunday of Lent, Year A

Turning Stones into Bread

As we come now to the first full week of Lent, it is as though we leave the anteroom, so to speak, and go forward into the unfolding weeks of this great season of grace. We look at what the Church offers us in her liturgy as material for growth. We see there a most loving Mother; but, as the true Mother she is, a very plain-spoken Mother, she takes us in the First Reading back to the fall of man. We see our first parents in the Garden. We see them making the mistakes that we make. They are proud, they are self-willed, and very particularly they do not accept the responsibility for their decisions. Adam, rather than taking the blame himself, blames his beloved helpmate. Eve, rather than asserting the beautiful strength that is in a woman to bear suffering, places the blame that justly belongs to her on the serpent. In the readings of the Mass, the Church herself is speaking to us very directly, as is God himself.

What is the Church asking us to do in Lent? To face the reality of ourselves. Adam could have said, "I am the head of this house. I should not have done this. I am the one at fault. I should have been an inspiration and direction for my wife." Eve could have said, "I was proud and I was weak and I dragged someone else into my weakness." So in this reading Holy Mother Church says, "Please let us face the reality of ourselves, because without doing that we cannot go forward."

The second thing the Church is showing us in this reading is what one person could do, what Adam could have done, what Eve could have done, and what each of us could do. Then she is showing us what follows on this: how we can help one another to be holy. Eve could have been inspired by Adam's right and humble answer. Surely she would have felt within her a great desire to rise to the same height of noble honesty.

Then we move on to the Gospel where the temptations of Christ in the desert are put before us, the three temptations that are before all creatures: carnality, presumption, and domination. How wonderfully this could be turned around for us by taking those invitations from the mouth of Satan and putting them in an inviting way into the mouth of Christ. Each one of us has many stones in her life—the stones of failure, the stones of misunderstanding, the stones of hurt. Our dear Lord says by his grace, particularly in this season, "Command these stones to become loaves of bread" (see Mt 4:3). These stones seem to impede us in our "nice" little plan to be holy. We are going to be so charitable, except someone upsets us. We are going to be understanding, except someone hurts us, and all down the line. These are stones, and we allow them to cause us to stumble on the way. Turn them into bread. How shall one be like the meek and humble Christ if one does not humble herself? How shall one be like the suffering Christ if one does not take the stones of suffering and turn them into the fullness of his divine intention that we should be holy?

I hope you will take this thought, which I dare to say is his thought, and make it your own, because I can see what a difference it makes. We do not have to deny the stones in our lives. All of us have hurts to bear, misunderstandings to suffer, difficulties in doing the penances we should do, difficulties in keeping on the path of fidelity: the stones of our fallen nature, the stones of our moods, the stones of our disappointments. But they can be turned into bread, and this is what Jesus says to us. He doesn't say, "I'll take all of these stones away. Now, what do you really need? I know what you want—a lovely, flower-bordered path to sanctity." No, he does not take the stones away, but he can show us how to turn them into bread. The hurts become the very things that unite us to the suffering and much-hurt Christ. The misunderstandings that make us stumble and fall are the very things that can unite us to him who was never completely understood by anyone, not even by his mother. Let us turn the stones into bread and not fool ourselves that, if only these stones were gone, we would be so holy. Rather, let us listen to his voice saying to us, "Command that these stones become loaves of bread." And then we can do it.

The second temptation can be transformed: "If you are the Son of God, throw yourself down; for it is written,

'He will give his angels charge of you', and 'On their hands they will bear you up, lest you strike your foot against a stone'" (Mt 4:6). Sometimes, perhaps often, we are afraid to take a plunge, to jump off, so to speak, the edge of this cliff where we know there is a certain safety. But we want to go forward into the unknown of the day's opportunities for sanctity, knowing we need not be afraid to jump off the comfortable cliff, knowing that not only do his angels have charge of us, but he has charge of us. When he asks us to do what seems impossible to our little minds, to our little cowardly hearts, we know God himself has charge of us, and so we can leap forward into what he asks of us. When he asks of us what seems difficult, whether large or small, he is always with us, and he will indeed keep us in all the ways on which he asks us to walk.

Then there is the third temptation: "All these I will give you, if you will fall down and worship me" (Mt 4:9). What a transformation it would be to understand these words as being said to us by Jesus: "Do not fall down before your hesitancies and your cowardice. I will give you joy and strength and perseverance if you fall down before me to adore my word and my will. All of the joys that ever could be, all of the peace that could ever be, all of the satisfaction beyond what you could ever imagine, all of these I will give you, if falling down you will adore me. Adore my will in all things, believe in all faith and adoration that whatsoever I ask of you is best for you."

I hope this will become a help to you in your prayer as it has already become to me: to take these terrible words of the Prince of Darkness and, in an entirely different way, put them on the divine lips of the King of Light. In all that lies before us during Lent of mortification, of disappointment, of sacrifice, he is saying, "Turn these stones into bread; grow stronger." When we want to say, "That is too much. I can't do that; that is beyond me", he is saying, "I have charge of you to keep you in all your ways that are my ways. There is nothing to be afraid of; you can do it." When we sometimes delude ourselves with a false humility, telling ourselves, "Oh, that is presumptuous. I could never take the dominance over my life", he says, "All of these things I will give you: the strength, the purpose, the new vision, the sweeping vision of your life if, instead of stumbling before your own weakness, you fall down before me and adore."

❧

First Sunday of Lent, Year B

True Self-Denial

The Church is a very vibrant Mother, and she shows us how happy she is about Lent. All through her liturgy there is this mood: something wonderful can happen. All of her prayers and directives are saying, "Please let it happen. Please allow it to happen." We are called to a glorious festival of love—to be spiritually dizzied with the fact that this is how much God has loved us. Surely we shall all look at the crucifix with a new vision, a deepened understanding that he really did this, he loved us this much. If we focus our thoughts on this reality we cannot be grudging. We cannot look at the crucifix and say, "This is too hard to do. This is too painful."

Holy Mother Church speaks of self-denial, of coming out of self to Christ, and we know what we mean when we set this program for ourselves in Lent. Yet, we must go beyond that understanding, which is true, to the deeper understanding that when we speak of denying ourselves, what we are really denying is a self that has gone awry, not our true selves. When we speak of the need not to be focused on self but on God, again we know what we mean. But in a much deeper meaning, our inmost self is where God is. It is when we are looking to the right and the left of self, so to speak, that we are not focused on that inmost self, on that inmost point of our being where God is, that inner court of our hearts where God is. Often I am out in the field, not in the inner court. This is our goal: not being focused on aberrations of self, but on the self that is God's idea of each of us.

From this viewpoint we see how, in our very efforts to serve ourselves, we are always disserving ourselves on every level: the physical level, the level of the heart, the level of thought, the level of emotions. For example, we try to make ourselves very comfortable. Who wants to kneel a little longer when we can collapse into a more comfortable position? God's comment on this is that we are more and more uncomfortable because we become softer in our self-seeking all the time. The dark reward of trying to do less and less is that we can do less and less and we have less and less taste for doing more. But, oh, there is a wonderful antithesis to that: the more we do, the more we exact of ourselves on any level, the more we can do. The more penance we do, the more penance we *can* do. Isn't that wonderful? The more we deny the aberrations of self, the more we can serve the great self that God thought worth creating.

We see this if we are indulging our emotions: I feel irritable, and I show I am irritable. I am willful, and I show that I am willful. And I am not happy. These are always expressions of unhappiness. Anger, unleashed passion, is never the expression of a happy person. Nor is there ever an expression of happiness from a proud person. Who are the happy ones? The humble ones of the earth. The ones who are always surprised at any gift, at any grace, amazed that they should be loved by God and others, that they should be forgiven, that they should be put up with. You can extend the long litany for yourself.

So, let us set out to deny our self-gone-wrong, and let us serve that inmost self where God is, where God's original idea of us is found. There is in our hearts that original innocence which he put there, and the clear vision that knows what is for our happiness, what is for our best good.

Let us reach out eagerly for the myriad occasions that God will give us to deny ourselves because they are graces that are beautiful and blessed. May we set out on this great adventure of Lent as persons denying the self that has "lost its looks", in order to bring it back to the inmost point of being where God asks for all the room.

First Sunday of Lent, Year C

Transformation

Surely a kind of awe comes over our hearts as we realize that this Lent, ripe with grace, is spread out before us. What are we going to do with it? Forty days seems a long time, but we know how swiftly they will go, and how swiftly the opportunities to grow in the love of Jesus crucified will come and will go.

At Matins during the week before Ash Wednesday, we read a sentence that shook me with its impact: "Allow God to transform you." God, the all-powerful, wants to transform us. We cannot do it by ourselves. We know how weak we are. We know our resources are quite insufficient for our ideals and our hopes, but he is all-sufficient. We know what he wants, and deep in our hearts we know what he wants changed in us. It is not that we have to sit down and think, "I wonder what could possibly be changed in me for the better." We do know. But the power is his, and our power is to allow God to transform us. A staggering phrase: allow the all-powerful God to make us holy; allow the all-powerful God to carry out his eternal plans for us.

Let us consider together: What is transformation? It is

literally being "carried over". It is not being changed in the sense that I no longer have my own identity, because that is a gift of God to me, or that I am no longer this particular individual person, for that is who he created me to be. God has an ideal of us. I am transformed into the form of his ideal of me. This is the person who was formed in his divine mind and brought into physical being. By our faults, our sins, our weaknesses, our failings, our failures to respond to grace, we have let the form grow nebulous, or we have let it become weakened and twisted. In Lent, God wants to carry us back to the fullness of his original idea of us. This is transformation. How often we have very sincerely made resolutions. We do want to change; we do want to go back, so to speak, to what we should be, to God's ideal of us; and often we are not very strong about getting there. But God is waiting to transform us, if we allow him.

One can even say, as daring as it sounds, that we need to allow the all-powerful God to do his will, for we can inhibit the will of almighty God. He wills our holiness; he wills the idea he has for us in this Lent. To each of us it is given to allow God to do what he wants to do, to allow God to do what he wills to do, to allow God to carry us over into his idea and his ideal and his divine hope. Let us be determined to allow God to transform us. Often this will involve things much harder than our own ideas. It is very good to make some very particular Lenten resolutions, but then we have to allow God to keep *his* Lenten resolutions for us. He has Lenten hopes for us. He has an idea of what he wants to find in us by Holy Week, by Easter. It is up to us to allow him.

Let us search the Mass readings for what God wants to tell us about transformation. Today we read the Gospel of the temptations of our dear Lord. We can look at these for a moment and ask how we apply them to ourselves. The devil appealed to our Lord's human weakness: "Command this stone to become bread" (Lk 4:3). The devil doesn't ever ask us to turn stones into bread, because he knows our limitations very well. But he does invite us to turn good opportunities into lost ones: "Oh, don't bother with that. It is not so important." Or, "Someday I will do that."

We get things out of proportion. When we are in an airplane thousands of feet above the earth, how small and how endearing the things of earth look. They look like little toy houses and little toy cars on the road. We do not see them that way when we are in the midst of them. But when we allow God to give us an ascended view, our vision is transformed and we see the smallness of the things of which we sometimes make so much, so that we do not see the greatness of the truly large things. We want to see things in proportion to God. In proportion to God, how big is this thing? Am I trying to look at it from a prayerful point of view, an ascended view, of what is large to God and what is small? I ask you to linger on that in your own prayer.

The second temptation was pride. We are on familiar ground here, because we are often tempted to pride.

In what way? It seems a cruel phrase but it can be true: in worshipping my own ideas, my own plans, my own decisions, my own determinations for what I want in a situation. Worshipping ourselves instead of worshipping the Lord of Lords and serving him alone, we are often serving ourselves, which in this sense means to disserve ourselves.

Then the devil tempted our dear Lord to presumption. "Throw yourself down." What is our presumption? It is the opposite of this classic temptation that the Gospel puts before us: the presumption that I can "get by". I don't do anything heinously wrong, but I don't do anything gloriously good, either. I go along from day to day. I do my work and I show up at Mass. I'm getting by. But I am not getting anywhere. When I am just getting by, the presumption is that this is enough. Along with that is the supine wishing, not a willing: "Yes, I would like to be holy. That is a nice idea." It never moves forward with force and continued intent. It is a presumption that a wishy-washy getting by is enough. It is not enough. Our own selves, if we listen, will tell us this, because we are never gloriously happy when we are just getting by. Each one of us is created with full potential for holiness in God's plan. Isn't that overwhelming? The so-called little things of every day are the opportunities to achieve that transformation into the fullness of God's plan for us.

The prophet Joel has told us about the One who transforms us. What is he like? Is this a powerful, frightening figure? He describes him for us: "slow to anger, rich in kindness, and relenting in punishment" (Joel 2:13, NAB). If we want to be transformed into that image of God who is rich in kindness, then we have to learn anew to be slow to anger, slow to be irascible, slow to be irritable. We have to be quick to overlook, quick to forgive. We find him all-patient. God doesn't give up. He is so patient. Why am I so slow to be patient? When I think how patient God has been with me, is it possible that I am impatient with circumstances, with persons, with arrangements? Is this possible? We come now in Lent to be transformed into an image of God's patience, his graciousness, his appreciation. God appreciates our poor little efforts to be what he gives us the power to be. He gives us the strength to be what we should be, and then he is so appreciative if we reach out to take and use the alms.

God shows us in this Gospel that the temptations of the devil can be resisted. I'm sure a shiver goes through each one of us as we read, "When the devil had ended every temptation, he departed from him until an opportune time" (Lk 4:13). The devil is not imitable in anything except his perseverance. The devil never gives up, ever. He is tireless in wanting to achieve what he wants to achieve in us: our downfall, our deformation instead of our transformation.

We know that none of us is exempt from temptation, and we know that at certain times in our dear Lord's human life he was tempted. He may have been tempted to regret and to stop the flow of his miraculous giving when the nine cured lepers did not come back. It was such an intimate sharing of our Lord when he revealed that he was hurt that they didn't even thank him. "Were not ten cleansed? Where are the nine?" (Lk 17:17).

We see how he was tempted to sadness and disappointment when he proclaimed the Eucharist and almost everyone turned away except his own little band. They did not believe although they saw his power. They believed he could raise people from the dead, and they believed he could cure incurable illnesses. They had seen it. But their faith stopped at a certain point. It was truly an incredible thing he was saying. But wasn't it an incredible thing to say to a dead man, "Get up"? He shows how hurt he was, how tempted he was to sadness, when he looked to his apostles and said, "Will you also go away?" (Jn 6:67). "Will you also hurt me, disappoint me as they are doing, those you now see from the back?"

We know very well how he was tempted to discouragement when he wept over Jerusalem. He wasn't just weeping very softly. He cried out loud: "Jerusalem, Jerusalem, you who kill the prophets and stone those sent to you, how many times I yearned to gather your children together, as a hen gathers her young under her wings, but you were unwilling!" (Mt 23:37, NAB). That is so tremendously moving. When we see the weeping of a strong person, our hardness, our false strength, and our strong pride are melted down. If we linger at the weeping of Christ, our pride will be softened. How many times have we acted as though we were unwilling in the little things that were asked, the responses, the opportunities?

He was tempted to discouragement. We see over and over in the Gospel that he was tempted to discouragement, even in his dying cry on the Cross, "My God, my God, why have you forsaken me?" (Mt 27:46). His human cry was followed immediately by a supreme act of entrustment, "Father, into your hands I commit my spirit!" (Lk 23:46). A marvelous thing, isn't it? By human standards, this is a complete *non sequitur*. This is a marvelous exposition of the humanity and the divinity of Christ.

Like Jesus, we can be led through temptation to the height of total trust in God. Let us allow him to transform us. Let us say to God, "Yes, you may do it. I give you the permission of my created will to transform me."

Recognition

WE TEND TO THINK of Judgment as something that comes after death. But God is judging us now: on how we lived this morning, what we did at our work, how much attention we gave to it, how much love we showed to our family. He is the judge of the living. We find the Church today pointing out all those around us: the hungry, the thirsty, the naked, and the prisoners. Christ is saying, "You did this to me." The ones who served others say in wonder, "When did we see you?" He answers each one, "Truly, I say to you, as you did it to one of the least of these my brethren, you did it to me" (Mt 25:40). What a thought that is!

Then we look at it from the dark side, the negative side, of those who were right there to excuse themselves: "We didn't see you hungry. We didn't see you thirsty. We would never have treated you like that. Never, never, never." He says, "You didn't do it to those around you, so you didn't do it to me, either." The Gospel is saying that this is the judgment—and the only judgment.

What are we hungry for? Primarily, every human heart is hungry for love. Love is the menu for everyone. Without love no one can rightly live or truly exist. We know it has been proven scientifically in modern times that infants will not grow if they are not loved. We all need this menu of love. Each one has her own particular hunger for love, and we must learn how to present love to each one. This is a wonderful thing, a thrilling thing to do, because it is an image of how God deals with us. He deals differently with each person. He has made no two alike. It is a wonderful challenge, how to feed each one.

Then Jesus talks about the thirsty. He draws into the Kingdom those who gave a drink to those who were thirsty. He condemns and casts into the eternal fire those who refused drink to the thirsty. What is the thirst that we have? Is it not for inspiration? We all need inspiration. On the material level, a person can go longer without food than without water. Famine causes terrible physical anomalies in the body, but thirst drives people crazy: their minds can no longer function. And so we need that inspiration from others all the time. We make our resolutions, we have a high ideal, and then we fall slack again. We need to have that inspiration coming to us; we need to see in one another the living example of the way we want to be. He is asking: Do you satisfy the thirst of others by your example?

Then he talks about the stranger. We all need a welcome. We need to be told again and again that we are welcome. This is part of the Gospel. We give that welcome by understanding. When we are understood, we are no longer strangers. And yet, at the core of understanding one another is accepting not to understand some things. I think this is sometimes the profoundest understanding. Maybe I don't understand why a person reacts as she does, why she does some things. But I am willing to welcome her without being able to follow a set of norms about her. This is a paradox: that I understand sometimes by being willing not to understand. I will not let her be a stranger. We do not let others be strangers simply because we do not understand the language they are speaking.

The next point is about clothing the naked. We need clothes. That is something very deep in us, ever since the first fall of man. It was the first thing Adam and Eve were aware of in their fallen condition; part of the penance of sin was being less at ease with their beautiful bodies, and thus feeling the need to cover them. And so we have a horror of being unclad. God has, so to speak, respected that need, and it has come to have its beautiful aspects, too, aside from the penitential shame with which it began. We show respect to the body by clothing it. This is what we must always be doing, putting the cloak of ourselves—our own cloak—around each other. It is such a humiliating thing to be unclad. We know that spiritually, emotionally, we are so poor in that way. Our poor little faults are so exposed before one another, and the more we try to hide them, the more naked we become. We are always to be covering over one another's weakness. We don't call a thing right that is wrong. But how do we cover it over? We think of the sons of Noah (see Gen 9:19–25). We remember that Noah was inebriated and that he was lying there, slumbering, and that he was unclad. One son pointed out the nakedness, and this was true. His father was drunk, and his father was naked. The other sons not only covered their father, but they walked backwards so as not to see him in this condition. When they saw their father at fault, they didn't lose their reverence. It seemed almost to deepen, in their need to cover over their father. God blessed them and all their progeny after them. So we are always to be covering one another, to be wrapping the cloak of ourselves around another, not ever staring at faults, as the son whose progeny was cursed stared at the faults of his father.

Next, the Lord talks about those who are sick, who are ill, and their need to be comforted. How much we need comfort from one another. We have that languor that comes to us all sometimes in our spiritual lives, what the desert fathers called "weariness in well-doing": we get tired of trying. We become like a small child. We're tired of doing what is right, and we become languid. When people are very languid, sometimes the doctor has to prescribe a remedy. Circumstances vary: one is languishing, and another has the enthusiasm; then when she is languishing, another has the enthusiasm. That is the wonder of our communal life. It is part of God's mercy, too—we don't all fall spiritually sick at the same time, so that everybody is in the infirmary, while nobody is up and about. We know, each of us, how we need encouragement. Whenever we see the evidence of languor, we bring our smile, our encouragement, our enthusiasm.

Lastly, the Lord talks of those who are in prison. He beckons into the Kingdom those who went and visited the prisoners, and he sends into the eternal fire those who did not go to those who were in jail. He says, "I was in prison, and you did not visit me. Depart from me." We are sometimes locked into prisons that we have built ourselves. When we see someone trapped in a spiritual prison, we can't wait for her to be released, but we must go to visit the one who is imprisoned in confusion and emotional tangles. We don't wait and say, "Yes, I'll see her as soon as she gets out; after she has served her term, I'll be there." No, we go to visit.

The Gospel tells us that this is where the King is: in the one who is hungry, who is thirsty, who is naked, who is ill, who is in prison. We can see that the whole point of this Gospel is: Did you recognize me, or did you not recognize me? Let us pray it penetrates through our poor little skulls that we are doing this to Christ or withholding it from Christ.

Tuesday of the First Week of Lent

The Three Stages of Contrition

We want to consider the stages of contrition bringing us to true conversion. It is significant that the feast of the Annunciation usually occurs during the Lenten season, for our Lady, though she herself was not in need of conversion, teaches us so much about the right response to our heavenly Father. We can reflect on the thought that the Yes of our Lady at the Annunciation was not yet complete in the sense that, although everything was at that moment totally given, every complete Yes led to a more complete Yes, as she saw what more God wished her to do.

This relates to what I wish to present for our pondering—something very precious to me—the story of David: David the chosen of God and David a flagrant sinner, David of the singing heart and David the weak one. We see the three stages of contrition very clearly in his story. The first incident in which David came to understand contrition was when the prophet Nathan came and spoke to him of his sin. He is confronted by Nathan with the full horror of what he has done. We are familiar with the passage (2 Sam 12:1–25) in which Nathan tells a story about a rich man who had everything and a poor man who had one little ewe lamb that was so precious to him. It was his whole love. It was like a child to him. Then the rich man, wanting to feed a visitor, took that ewe lamb from the poor man. David reacts in highly dramatic style. He says, as we would put it in modern jargon, "Let me at him!" David condemns this monster of selfishness, this flagrant sinner. Then comes the critical moment in David's life. We can see the scene, can we not? David fuming, perhaps waving both arms in the air with clenched fists: "Just name him; tell me where he is. I'll take care of this fellow." And there is Nathan, looking at him, without pointing at him, very quietly saying, "You are the man."

This is the critical point. David had choices before him. David could have said, "How dare you speak like that to the king!" David could have removed Nathan from the scene in one way or another, because the prophet was telling David a truth that he did not wish to face. We wonder if there was a hush at that moment as never before, a deafening silence. David is caught; which way will he go? Will he turn his fuming now on Nathan? Will he turn from the truth with a great show? Or will he accept what Nathan is saying: "You are the one"?

David accepts this, and this was the complete Yes of David, the Yes that we are all called to make when God confronts us with the truth. At the Annunciation, God sent his messenger to our Lady. He sends his messengers to us as well. In a sense, we can say that our life is populated with angels. In every situation there is a messenger saying something to us. As often as we are unwilling to face ourselves, the real reason for our wrong action, our immaturity, our passion, there is someone saying, "You are the one. It's not the situation; it's not the circumstance; it's not this other person. You are the one."

We want to deepen the desire to be able to say, "Yes, I am the one", because this is where grace is found. A complete Yes changed David's whole life. Because it was so complete, God could lead him on to a more complete Yes.

Then we see the second stage of contrition, for which he was prepared by saying, "Yes, I am the one." David is fleeing from his son Absalom, surrounded by his royal bodyguards. He is the king, and no one is going to accost the king. Then this fellow, Shimei, comes out from the forest and begins throwing stones at him. Shimei is cursing him and saying, "Begone, begone, you man of blood, you worthless fellow!" (2 Sam 16:7–11). The royal bodyguard says with courtly elegance, "Let me go over and take off his head." The scene is as highly dramatic as anything can be, in a sense tragic, but not without humor. David says, "Let him alone and let him curse, for the LORD has bidden him."

By this time David, having accepted the truth that Nathan had spoken, is able to see deeper into truth. David is not making a great show of "Yes, I'm no good and I never was any good. I've shed all this blood." He knows that what Shimei is saying is not factually true, but he penetrates to the truth of what God is saying. And so he says, "Let him alone. Perhaps God has told him to curse David." David is now aware of his sinfulness and, far from debilitating him, this awareness gives him strength, the strength that contrition always brings. God was offering him a penance, which he accepted and to which he gives now a second complete Yes, in a sense more complete than the first. He does not trifle by excusing himself with, "I didn't do any of those things that he said", but he looks deeper and sees himself as one entirely worthy of having stones thrown at him. He says, "Let him alone. Perhaps God has told him to do this and to say this. Don't you touch him." At this dramatic moment, he accepts Shimei as he had accepted Nathan—as a messenger of God.

Out of this second complete Yes, he can be lifted into that third stage of his contrition in the grief that he feels for perhaps the deepest wrong that could ever be done to a parent: betrayal by his own child. David is elevated to such a height of grief, not for himself, but entirely for Absalom, because he has been purified in these two preceding confrontations with the truth about himself. And so from his heart, purified by truth, by humility, by acceptance, comes one of the greatest cries in the Old Testament, something I can never hear or read without feeling the smart of tears behind my eyelids. It is so absolutely pure. He sees the whole truth. Absalom is the one to be pitied. He does not cry out in a way that we could well understand and that would not be blameworthy: "My son, my own son has betrayed me. Who could suffer more than this? I brought him up, I trained him, I taught him, I guided him. This traitorous son of mine, he would like to see me off the scene: he would like my throne, my authority for himself." But David, purified by truth and converted in his heart, thinks only of Absalom and utters that great cry: "O my son Absalom, O Absalom, my son, my son!" (2 Sam 19:4). He grieves, not for David betrayed by the son, but for the betrayer. Surely David, weeping up in that tower, is finding excuses for Absalom: "He's so young. He got carried away with the passion of ambition. He was ill-advised. Perhaps I didn't guide him right. Perhaps I wasn't firm enough with him. Perhaps in my love for him, I did not take a firmer stand with him." We can hope that, by the foreseen merits of David, Absalom was saved.

In the stages of contrition, if we refuse the first truth we shall not be able to penetrate into the unfolding truth. We shall be forever excusing ourselves, blaming others, resting at the surface of things. Nor will we be able to attain that purification that is always concerned for the other and pertains to the very heart of our life. On the other hand, each time that we confront the truth and say, "Yes, I am the one who is lacking. I am the one who deserves to be reprimanded by God. I would be well served for all of my sins and my faults by having stones thrown at me", we are able with grace to let fall away the petty need to justify ourselves, to bring in all the extenuating circumstances. We are able to say with David that perhaps God has told someone to say this to me. Finally, even beneath his tears for Absalom, there had to be an indescribable depth of Joy in David's heart that he had been liberated from David. He was all for the other.

Wednesday of the First Week of Lent

Have Mercy, O God

Today's Responsorial Psalm is Psalm 51, the "Miserere" —perhaps the greatest poem of repentance ever written. We see what King David, the great penitent, is saying in his confession. To rely absolutely on God's forgiveness is to recognize the necessity to forego despair, which can be an easy exit from effort. There is no sin that is greater than God's forgiveness. The great saint of Carmel, Thérèse of Lisieux, says, "If I had committed all the sins which can be committed, I would go, my heart broken, to repent and throw myself into the arms of Jesus, for I know how much he cherishes the prodigal child who returns to him." This was someone who understood contrition.

We begin in the English (Grail) translation by saying, "Have mercy on me, God, in your kindness", but what the Latin really means is that I need something superlative. I need something unlimited. I don't need a small bit of kindness, but your mercies are so great, so beyond number, *multitudinem*, that there is still something left for me. Maybe I think that I've exhausted your kindness in a day, but then I see it's multitudinous. It cannot be numbered. It's so great that there is room for me. When you have spent it all, there are still leftovers for me.

It is significant that when David makes his confession, already he is speaking of Joy. I counted them up: one, two, three, four, five, six, seven, eight expressions of Joy in this clearest expression of a good confession. We have *gaudium*, joy; *laetitiam*, happiness; *exsultabunt*, my bones are going to dance around for joy. A wonderful picture! We think of a skeleton, a morbid figure, rattling its bones in nightmares and haunted houses, but David is saying, "My bones are dancing around for joy."

David makes a very clear statement here. His focus is on himself in confrontation, but outside himself in purpose. He is seeking forgiveness, but he is full of hope, and so he says, "You don't despise a broken heart", *cor contritum et humiliatum*. *Contritum* is such a rich word. It means literally, "broken into pieces". It does not mean pulverized. A thing pulverized has really lost its identity. If we try to pulverize ourselves with self-blame, with self-abuse, with denigration of self, we are excused from effort. This is an escape.

On the other hand, a broken object can be put back together. The worse the breakage, the greater is the need for a truly expert artist to do this. The more sinful we are and the more the heart is broken into pieces by the realization of this, the more we need the Master Artist, the faster do we run to God to put us back together. Something that is broken into pieces is not something standing tall looking down on other objects. It is humbled, *humiliatum*. This is what catches the eye of God. He doesn't look away. God comes to the heart that is broken and humbled.

One could dare to say in our faltering human language that God is overcome by humility because he sees in it the image of his own Divine Son, who clearly said, "I am meek and humble of heart." So when the Eternal Father sees humility in us he is deeply moved (see Hos 11:8). He sees his Divine Son shining through our sinfulness, our faultiness, our clumsiness, our perseverance in mediocrity, and the sight of him is irresistible.

Let us look briefly at some of these wonderful phrases in the "Miserere". The English, "blot out all my iniquity", is very, very weak in comparison with *dele iniquitatem meam*. We would say colloquially, "knock it out completely". This is not a matter of something that can just be blotted. This is something that needs force. It needs to be destroyed, "destroy my sinfulness". Then he says, *amplius*, do this more and more. "Don't give me, as it were, a perfunctory washing. Keep at this, keep sprucing me up, keep cleansing me, God, because there are layers and layers of iniquity in me, and it is only when one is taken away that I can see the others." When great masterpieces of art are restored, layers and layers of the overlay are removed before the real painting is found. So it is with our sins. We ask God to take off one coat after another of sin and pretense until his real image is visible again.

David continues, "I know my sin. I do not underestimate it by excuse. I do not exaggerate it into despair, but I know it in truth." Then there is a wonderful theology of what sin is. In the English translation we say, "My sin is always before me." The Latin says, *Peccatum meum contra me est semper* (my sin is always against me). It's not in front of me; it's against me, *contra me*; it's fighting me. David is saying, "It is you I have sinned against, and this evil is always against me. My sinfulness is always there trying to defeat me; from the beginning it is against me. It was against Adam and Eve. It kept fighting against them so that they would not confess in truth. They resorted to excuses. Come and shoot down the enemy, this sin of mine, which is always against me."

He goes on to say, "You have loved the truth." A true examination of conscience faces the truth without diminution or disproportion or exaggeration because God loves the truth. "I am such a sinner, and I have done wrong." This was the truth, and there wasn't all that much room for David to exaggerate. These were terrible things that he had done: adultery, murder, lying, treachery, the utmost self-indulgence of both body and mind, the debasement of his own heart. Yet he says what every true penitent will come to say: "But you will wash me and I will be whiter than snow."

David marvels that God will not make him crawl away in self-hatred for the rest of his life. He says, "You will give me *gaudium et laetitiam*, joy and happiness." That's when he comes out with this marvelous phrase, "my bones are going to dance around". These bones that have been broken and humbled now begin to dance around: *exsultabunt ossa humiliata*. He says, "My tongue will rejoice", *exsultabit lingua mea*. So while my bones are dancing around with the joy of being forgiven, my tongue will be a tongue that says kind words, that brings joy to others.

Then he says, "Now, God, let's forget it. Don't look at it anymore, *averte faciem tuam* (turn away your face), and let us start over." I think these are words God loves to hear. God always responds, "Yes, let's start over. After all, I did know this would happen; I did foresee it. Let's start over."

He ends with a little prayer that shows that only those who really accept forgiveness can deal very familiarly with God. David says, *Benigne fac, Domine,* "Be kind to me, Lord. You and I both know my history, and I have this feeling that I might get into trouble again. Help me, O God, for I want to change."

Thursday of the First Week of Lent

The Elements of Confession

When one is contrite, one has to say so. This is always the driving force of true contrition, that I must say I am sorry. We see this very clearly in David, whom we have been considering as an example of contrition. There are three elements that must be present if we are making a true confession of our sins in the Sacrament of Reconciliation or in our prayer before God. Interestingly enough, I find myself with alliteration in these elements without searching at all for any device like this. Confession must be factual. It must be focused. And it must be full of faith.

We can be nonfactual through the excuse: "Yes, I did this, but it was because of this situation, it was because of this circumstance, it was because of this person." The world is full of excusers, and often we add to the plenitude of those who always dilute the fact or ascribe the fact to someone else or to the situation or to circumstances. That's obvious enough. But it is also true that we can depart from factuality just as disproportionately by enlarging on facts until they have lost the outline of truth, by making this sin appear so much worse that we bring ourselves to the stage of thinking that this sin cannot possibly be forgiven. Then we are left with the conclusion: "I'm going to go right on being like that. This is so big, this is so deep in me, this has so embroiled my being that I can't be any different. I'm just no good." This is always another way of saying, "And that's the way I'm going to continue to be." These two evasions of fact that seem so utterly opposite are part of the same lack of truth. A real confession faces the fact as it is, whereas I can continue in my own unconverted way if I consider sin to be less than it is or to be beyond the power of God to forgive.

The second element of confession is focus. A true and availing confession can never be focused on ourselves. In the light of God's truth we confront ourselves, but we do not stay with our misery, because to stay there will either drive us to despair or to a commitment to untruthfulness. We focus on God, the forgiving One. Strangely, we sometimes find this hard to do. We almost fear focusing on God. Why is that? It is because focus on God drives us to change. Focus on ourselves does not. It can make us more untruthful all the time, more sly, more evasive, more unreal. We need to focus on God, whom we have never taken by surprise, who loves us not because we are so good but because he is so good. This is all-demanding. We must focus on God as the One who loves us and the One who, we might dare to say, has been driven to forgive us. So driven was he by his love that he sent his only Son to suffer and die for us that he might redeem us. When we focus on that, we are obliged to change.

In human relationships if someone were to say, "I've had enough. That's the end. Don't ever come back to me again. I've told you this often enough", this would certainly harden us. This would drive us to be worse than we ever were before, and induce despair. But most of us have experienced that tremendous casting down into humility by the one who always forgives us, the one who says, "Let's start over. Now that you've learned from this, let us go forward." This is what really impels us, urges us, incites us, because it humbles us. And only the humble can really go forward.

The third "F" is faith. Do we really believe that God can forgive us and, related to the second point, that God wishes to forgive us? We say this with great wonder: it is God's joy to forgive us. Although our fallen human nature is often proud, hard, and overbearing, we are not so utterly debased as to say to someone, "No, I will not forgive you." Would we think less of God? Will we not allow ourselves to be led into that mystery of God's rejoicing to forgive us? The figure that Jesus gives us is the Good Shepherd, but this is perhaps so familiar that we do not really understand. We have not pondered it profoundly enough. The picture has been put before us by artists of Christ the Good Shepherd with that sinning little sheep around his neck, or held in his embrace. It is obvious where that sinning little recovered sheep has been and what he's been doing. Yet he doesn't mind, because of where he is now. He has been saved, he has been wanted. God gives us the figure of his searching us out in his mercy, going into the brambles after the lost sheep. It is hard to go into brambles: one is scratched and torn and cut, and one grows tired. He goes out on the highways and byways and begs us to come in and be forgiven. This is the great invitation of the redeeming Christ: Come and be forgiven.

Friday of the First Week of Lent

❧

Amendment and Penance

It is of great spiritual benefit to avail ourselves of the Sacrament of Reconciliation often during this holy season, and so let us continue our consideration of this great gift ministered to us through our Holy Church. Just as there is no sacramental absolution without contrition and without the actual confession, so the Sacrament of Reconciliation is not valid unless we are determined to do penance and to amend our lives. To whom do we confess? To Almighty God. But we never sincerely confess to God what we have not first confessed to ourselves. The first confession is confessing to myself in true confrontation that I am guilty, I have sinned, I am at fault. If we do not have that first confession in the truth, that cleansing self-confrontation, we will not rightly confess to God. We cannot tell God anything he does not know, and we cannot rightly express to God what we have not expressed in truth to ourselves.

There is always the danger of the sacrament becoming routine: yes, we're sorry, and we receive a token penance. We bring our sins and failures, and the priest gives us some little prayer, some little consideration, some suggestion about a little sacrifice to make—a far cry from the public penitents who were not allowed in the church for a time and were given what we would consider towering penances to perform. We are sorry, we do our penance, and then that's it. We can almost forget the purpose of amendment, the lack of which invalidates the sacrament. This was a driving force in the lives of all the saints. The more one is contrite, the more one is driven to tell everyone, "I am sorry", the more there is purpose of amendment, the need to do penance, and an understanding of the real heinousness of sin. We could say that the one who perhaps has the least weight of personal sin in the eyes of God is the one who is most driven by an urge to repair.

If in all my life I had committed only one venial sin, there is need for me to make reparation all my life long, because I have offended an infinite God and I can never repair enough. My reparation, my amendment could never reach his infinity. That is why the Father sent his Son, who was the only one who could make adequate satisfaction. He balanced our sin against the infinite with his infinite reparation. Yet there must be cultivated in us that urge to reparation.

When I have acted very badly, hurting a person I love, the other person may say, "Oh, it's all forgiven. Let's forget it." There is a sense in which we do forget it, in which we are not bound and constricted by it. We go forward in love. But there is a beautiful, positive sense in which we must never forget it. It is the very opposite of brooding. It is a sense of needing to repair. When I am very much aware that I have hurt, disappointed, caused suffering to the one I love, I am so alert. What can I do? I want to show more love. I am more intent than ever on not disappointing this person again. I want to do this. I'm looking around for something to do. This is what is at the heart of reparation. It is a total belief in being forgiven; but the love of Christ urges me, I must do something. So a penance is given, and a penance must be done.

David was given a penance for his flagrant sins of adultery, murder, treachery, lying, and all the rest: God took the child of his sin. But there was another penance later on: David would not be allowed to build the temple. God had forgiven David absolutely, and David knew it, and he made this clear in the "Miserere". But God gave him a penance to be carried out, as if to say, "Yes, I will forgive you, but you will not build my temple. Your son will do this."

This brings us to the Church's teaching of the temporal punishment due to sin, which is not understood in our era. Similarly, there is a whole aberration of the very understanding of education in our times: we must never punish the child, never. So we raise up a whole generation of undisciplined, weak persons who have never had the advantage of being punished. *Punishment* is not an "in" word, but it remains an "in" word with God.

In the early chronicles of Franciscan history we are told that the friars ran to Francis to be corrected. They couldn't get there fast enough. They ran to be corrected and to be punished. They humbly begged for the gift of a penance. They had that purpose of amendment, that need to make reparation. It seems to me that temporal punishment due to sin is what we feel in our hearts when we have offended someone we love. It is not a brooding thing, not a constricting thing. Just the opposite, it is a liberating thing. It takes us out of ourselves. And so it is a wonderful thing.

It is a prayerful speculation to say that after Peter's denial, he came to our Lady for consolation. He knew he was forgiven. He was forgiven on a grand scale; he was made the first Pope, the rock on which the Church was built. But surely he bore in his heart always that temporal punishment due to his sin. We can picture our Lady saying, "What is the matter?" when he came weeping, and Peter saying, "I heard a rooster crow." It was always there, and it drove him on and on to such a climax that he not only wanted to suffer for the love of Christ, but at the end of his life he said, "I'm not even fit to die in the same position in which he died." The purpose of amendment had driven Peter so far that he went beyond saying, "Oh, if I could die just as he did, if I could be crucified". But he said, "No, I don't deserve to die the same way he died. Would you please crucify me upside down?" This is certainly the triumph of bearing the temporal punishment due to sin.

I want to make amends. The fact that I can never balance things out with an infinite God whom I have offended drives me all the more. Sometimes are we not best driven by impossibility, that urgency to love God with all our hearts? I am determined I will never offend him again, and yet I know I will. This urgency to do the impossible is at the heart of sanctity. A purpose of amendment is urgent: "I've got to make this right; I've got to balance this out." We read in the Scriptures that Christ bore the weight of our sins. The purpose of amendment makes us so eager to take on ourselves a little bit of the weight of the sins of all men from the beginning of time, to fill up in ourselves what has been left to us of the sufferings of Christ (see Col 1:24).

The test of the real penitent, who wishes to do penance and has a firm purpose of amendment, is obvious: this person is on the watch—tender, sensitive, and alert. This person is far from being hard and grim. One is sensitized to the need of the person one has offended. One sees things one would not have seen before: things to do, love to show. We will want to live in this high ambition: to ease the hurt of our Beloved.

Saturday of the First Week of Lent

The Rending of the Heart

The prophet Joel says, "Rend your hearts, not your garments" (Joel 2:13, NAB). During our Lord's Passion, we see the high priest rending his garments as though a terrible thing had been said, which demonstrated his hypocrisy and hatred of anyone who seemed to supersede him in his petty governance. Joel tells us to rend our hearts, not our garments. That seems a brutal thing to do: rend your heart, tear it apart. In a heart surgery, when a heart is invaded, it is torn by a surgeon's knife. We draw back, for this is a fearsome thing, requiring a long healing. Our dear Lord's heart was rent on the Cross very literally by the centurion's spear, and there came out blood and water. As a sign of his infinite love, there flowed out his very blood to the last drop of it, and there flowed out water, the sign of salvation.

The rending of the heart to which the prophet is inviting us is not fearsome but salvific. This is what we want to do in Lent: rend our hearts. When our hearts are rent, what is found? There was nothing found in the heart of Jesus but love and forgiveness. We need to rend our hearts to see what must be evicted from them. A person's heart can be rent with grief. Hopefully with the illuminations of Lent when we look into our own lives and our own failures and our own lack of response to grace and our infidelities and our pettiness, our hearts are rent with grief. That is a wonderful thing. We want to rend our hearts this Lent and see what is in them, dismissing from them, with the grace that will be given to do this, what does not belong in the heart of a Christian. Rend the heart with prayer, with penance, with love, to see, admit, and confess in the daylight of God's love what is there. We admit that there should be nothing in it but a hostel of love and giving; but if instead there are some little complaints, some little grudges, some little fault-findings, some pettiness, let us rend our hearts and get rid of these things with the power of Lenten grace that will be given to us.

Jesus tells us in today's Gospel that we are to be perfect as our heavenly Father is perfect (Mt 5:48). That is quite a program, isn't it? When we rend our hearts and empty from them what does not belong, then it is God who will make us perfect. For what is perfection? Is it not full contrition and full effort? Perfection for us can never mean, "I have never done anything wrong. I've never committed a sin. I've never committed a fault." Nor can we dare to say, although we would love to say it, we would love it to be true, "I will never commit a fault again." It is enough to desire with all my heart that I should never do it again. And then God can make perfect our imperfections.

On the human level, someone who is greatly gifted in

a certain field can make perfect the imperfections of another's work. A very great musician can perfect the imperfections of a lesser musician's work. A great writer can make perfect the imperfection of much poorer writing, and the same in all the arts. Should we think that God cannot do more, that God cannot make perfect?

In a Lenten reading at Matins Saint Athanasius tells us, "True joy, genuine festival, means the casting out of wickedness. To achieve this one must live a life of perfect goodness and, in the serenity of the fear of God, practice contemplation in one's heart." That is very inviting. I like the idea of true joy and I love the idea of a festival. But it means, we are told, the casting out of wickedness. How do we do this? What are the means? Striving to live a life of perfect goodness is as far as our poor little humanity can get.

It is quite shattering to say, and yet we all know that this is true: the little wickednesses of daily infidelity can be so inviting. They have ugly little faces, ugly little forms, but they can be so inviting. Yet goodness can come to be more inviting than any infidelity. How can that be? According to the measure we practice it. Sometimes a little child will say, "It's so hard to be good!" And so we have to practice. It is hard to become a concert pianist. It is hard to become an expert surgeon. It is hard to become an outstanding ballerina. We have to practice and practice and practice. If this is true of the worldly arts, it is more true of the art of spiritual fidelity. Sometimes in our slothfulness or our fear we are doing the equivalent of saying to God, "It's so hard." I think God says to us, "You don't practice enough."

We are not immaculately preserved from sin like our Lady. We are not all-holy like our Divine Savior, but this is our perfect goodness: always to be casting out what is wrong, finding our serenity in true fear of God.

SECOND WEEK OF LENT

Second Sunday of Lent, Year A

Clear Vision

THE SUNDAY LITURGY presents the Transfiguration Gospel, and if we little ones, instead of our enlightened Mother the Church, had selected the readings, we probably would not have picked this one. It seems an anticipation of Easter. What is this glorious, almost apocryphal message doing here for the second Sunday of Lent? We might think the Church is encouraging us, just as Jesus encouraged his apostles, and yet we pause there a moment. The encouragement he gave nearly frightened the wits out of them when he let his glory shine through. Often his gifts to us, which are meant to console and strengthen us, frighten the wits out of us, too. After the apostles had experienced what they saw and heard and had fallen down in fright, they looked up and saw Jesus—the Jesus whom they knew, the Jesus who ate with them, who walked with them, who put up with them, who was so patient with them, who reprimanded them and who forgave them. "They saw no one but Jesus only" (Mt 17:8).

We can turn that phrase like a diamond in our hands, looking at many facets of it, and especially as we apply it to our own lives: only Jesus. How often in the little or large difficulties we have, the little or large sufferings, we see just about everything but Jesus. Maybe we hear the thunder and smell the smoke and we are frightened by the sounds, the lightning, and the darkness. We do not see only Jesus, which would make everything different.

We think of that incident when the apostles are rowing hard against the wind in that not-very-seaworthy craft of theirs; he comes walking upon the water, and they think it is a ghost and they are frightened half out of their wits until they find out that it is Jesus. The storm doesn't matter then, and the danger doesn't matter. It is Jesus. He's coming, he's there (see Mt 14:24–33).

In joy, too, we are sometimes carried away and do not see Jesus, so the joy evanesces. We know that in sorrow we turn more easily to God than in joy. We can just rest in the joyous things without remembering to thank, or, more importantly, to look at him. For Jesus is at the center of every real joy. He is the meaning of all joy, and he is the explanation of all sorrow, of all suffering.

When we are not trying to see only Jesus, often there is no explanation for suffering. People without faith take their own lives, or they become violent toward others, or they literally go mad with suffering and sorrow because they are not seeing only Jesus. In a similar way, people can go excessively wild with pleasure because they have not seen the joy that is Jesus alone.

In the events of daily life, little and large things arise that are irritating, annoying, difficult to bear: the unintended slights, the misunderstandings that are a part of all human life. Through these situations our Lord is saying that he wants us to come closer to him. Sometimes we see everything under the sun except, so to speak, the Sun —Jesus. Let us try to look at Jesus. When we look up in sorrow or in joy to see Jesus, this by no means indicates that we do not see others. The marvelous paradox is that when we see only Jesus, then we see everyone else in all circumstances with true, clear vision.

As we know, physical astigmatism distorts vision. If we are not directing our vision toward Jesus, we can have spiritual astigmatism. We see the little things of daily life much larger than they really are. Sometimes they become so large that they are all we can see. They really are so small, but we don't have right spiritual vision. Our eyes are not trained on Jesus, and so these little things become so big, maybe impossible to respond to, impossible to handle. On the other hand, maybe the meaningful things of every day, the significant things for time and for eternity, the great, giant happenings in our life are seen with that blurred spiritual vision so that they don't look very important. They look quite small. This call to fidelity, this little hidden thing, appears so small; actually it is very large. It can be something that changes the whole course of our life.

Whenever we see only Jesus with that clear, focused vision on him, then we see all people and all things and all events and all happenings as they truly are. We don't see them with astigmatic vision. We don't see them distorted. We don't see them larger than they are; we don't see them smaller than they are. We don't see them all out of line on the page. We don't see them blurred. How often we see things with such blurry vision in the spiritual life! Let us strive for clear vision as we remember this Gospel. "They saw no one but Jesus only." Then they didn't have to be afraid. Then they could be encouraged, and they could realize he was right there. He was right there all the time. Because of that, after he had physically disappeared from their sight at the Ascension, they went on seeing only Jesus. How do we know that? Because they were martyred for him, because they spent themselves utterly for him. They saw only Jesus. If we see only Jesus, we will see many things we did not see before, and we will see all things differently.

Second Sunday of Lent, Year B

In Conversation with Jesus

In the Sunday liturgy, the First Reading recounts that most wonderful story of Abraham and the integrity of his faith. Our Lord calls, "Abraham!", and Abraham says, "Here am I!" (Gen 22:1). I thought of how these words must have delighted God. We are not called to such dramatic tests of faith. Yet what God gives to us *is* large because we are so small. How wonderful if God could hear from us always that "Here am I", in the expected or the unexpected. Abraham didn't say, "Well, what do you have on your mind, God?" He didn't say, "Explain it all to me", but just, "Here am I!" How we could glorify God by always giving this response!

The Church is calling us now to reflect deeply on Abraham, our father in faith. Abraham was the father of nations because he was a man of faith. God had already led Abraham a long way, and he had promised him a child and told him he would be the father of nations. We know Abraham was a nonagenarian and there was no child, and his wife was a nonagenarian and there certainly wasn't going to be any child. But Abraham just went on believing. We might think that was enough faith, and wish we had even that much. If only we could come to believe what is so easy to say—that nothing is impossible with God. But because Abraham went that far, he could go further. It is the same with us. When we make one response, we can go further. When we fail in one response, we backslide.

We trace, step-by-step, that most marvelous exposition of the integrity of faith. His faith was rewarded. He had the child. Against all laws of nature, the child was given. Then Abraham went off in faith with his "Here am I!" to find out what God's command meant. Abraham endured the greatest trial of faith, which was not "just" that God was asking the utterly impossible, but that God seemed to contradict himself: Isaac was the child of the promise, through whom Abraham would become the father of nations, and now God was asking that Isaac be sacrificed. For this, too, Abraham went forward and was ready. Abraham had that faith because he realized that Isaac was not his. Isaac was the child of his own flesh and blood, truly, but Abraham understood that Isaac was God's, not his. Isaac was at God's disposal.

He went forward in obedience. The hardest moment of all, perhaps even harder than lifting the knife, must have been when the child said, "Behold the fire and the wood; but where is the lamb for the burnt offering?" (Gen 22:7). This was surely the moment when Abraham's heart broke in faith, so that God might put it back together. He tied the child and lit the fire. We know that God then sent his angel to stay his hand.

Abraham was not asked to be ready for something he

knew all about, in the way that we say, "Be ready and dressed for this supper engagement which will begin at eight o'clock." No, he didn't know what he was supposed to be ready for. We want to ask ourselves, how ready are we? In our daily life we say we want to be holy; we say we want to grow. Are we ready for the little unexpected sacrifice asked of us? And is any real sacrifice ever expected? Is that not part of the nature of sacrifice, that perhaps it was not expected? How ready are we? How ready are we to be real?

We all have our Isaacs—some of them lofty, some of them pertaining to the promise, some of them wondrous, and some of them very little Isaacs indeed. I would ask that we look into our lives to see what perhaps ignominious little Isaacs we may have, or to look at all of the Isaacs and to examine whether we realize that they are not ours. Saint Paul says, "What have you that you did not receive? If then you received it, why do you boast as if it were not a gift?" (1 Cor 4:7). We want to enter more deeply into the mystery of poverty.

We can make an Isaac sometimes out of our work. It is wonderful to be attached to our work in the right way, in the sense that we love it. We give it all the energy and devotedness that we possibly can, in total fidelity. But we do not own it. We do not set up a kingdom in our work. We realize that at any moment this work could be taken from us, and we need to be ready to lift our hand with the knife, as did Abraham, because this Isaac of our work does not belong to us.

Sometimes our Isaac is a pet project. It may be a very good one, maybe a study project. It can be intense and very beneficial to the interior life, but it is not ours. If at any moment it should be said to us, "No, stop that, give it up. Turn it over to someone else. Throw it away", then we know the project does not belong to us.

We could go down a long list, but let me just mention here one Isaac that may escape our attention because we are so involved in it: the Isaac of our pet problem. Years ago there was a fad that I read about—people had what they called a "pet rock". You give a lot of attention to this rock, and you show it to people, and this is your pet. It's kind of silly, but it can be tragic. What is my pet rock, what is my Isaac-problem that I do not wish to have solved? I turn it upside down, I look at it from right to left, I pet my pet rock and think about it and take the burden of it upon myself. I will in no way sacrifice that problem. That pet rock of a problem has become my security. Perhaps people are blamed because of my pet rock, my pet Isaac-rock. This is a shivering thought. Our life can start revolving around our pet rock. No one may solve this, no one may dare to say, "You know, that is not much of a problem. It's not much of a pet. It really doesn't deserve all of that attention. Why don't you throw it away? Why don't you toss that pet rock out into the gravel path where it could be doing some good?" Let us joyfully give God our Isaac, whether it be our work, our project, our interest, our concern, or whether it be our pet rock of a problem.

Then, a word about the Tabor Gospel. I was newly impressed by the fact that Moses and Elijah were in conversation with Jesus. Let us be occupied always in being in conversation with Jesus. We know the deepest conversations are the wordless ones. We love that simple and profound word of Pope Saint John Paul II, "Let Jesus be the one to whom you talk the most." When we speak, let us speak to Jesus the most. We think with shame that in some of our little difficulties perhaps we speak to him the least, and talk to ourselves the most.

Moses and Elijah were in conversation with Jesus. They were speaking with him and they were with him, and that was the deepest conversation. Let us be found in conversation with Jesus. It is he alone who has the right word to respond to our questions. It is he alone who has the perfect questions, the piercing, saving questions to ask of us.

Second Sunday of Lent, Year C

A Cultivated Memory

The Sunday liturgy presents the strange Gospel of the Transfiguration—and by "strange" I do not mean only in its mysticism, high drama, and apocalyptic expression, but in its very placement at the heart of Lent. If we dull little people were composing the liturgy, we might not have placed it there; but since it does occur within the Lenten liturgy, we are enabled to see that our Lord's purpose in taking his intimates up on the mount with him was to give them something to remember in hard times. He knew what they did not know: that there were very suffering times ahead of them. Although he had already adverted to it, they were very assiduous in forgetting what he said. Peter had on one occasion told him, "God forbid, Lord! This shall never happen to you" (see Mt 16:22). Now the time had come, he felt, to fortify them with the vision of the enduring reality in the face of the stark, appalling realities that lay immediately before them in the terrible events of the Passion and crucifixion. He knew that, as all events end in time, these too would pass, although the Church would treasure them in her memory always. What would remain forever was the glory that the apostles glimpsed on Mount Tabor—and this was what he gave them to remember. In the dark hours immediately after the crucifixion when they had seen him apparently completely defeated, utterly weak, completely helpless, they must have remembered Tabor.

In the First Reading, too, the Church is giving us something to remember. God tells Abraham that his descendants will be as numerous as the sands on the seashore, more numerous than the stars in the firmament (see Gen 15:5). To Abraham, this didn't look very likely. There were many dark days for Abraham; he didn't become our father in faith effortlessly. Abraham had the greatest opportunity for faith that anyone could ever be given: God seemed to contradict himself. God had worked the miracle of sending the child of the promise, when Sarah was far past the normal age of childbearing; then God told Abraham to offer the child as a victim, to kill him. This was perhaps Abraham's greatest trial. For us, too, in our little ways, it can sometimes seem that God contradicts himself. He tells us to do something, and then it seems that he sets up all manner of obstacles. Yet God gave to Abraham the promise to remember; and Abraham must have had to recall it to mind many, many times. Did he think of it there on the mount of sacrifice? How many times he must have had to remember it, in order to become the great man that he was.

Memory gives us the opportunity for choice. We choose

what we want to remember and what we will remember. In the ordinary events of life, we can see the dark tendency in ourselves to make poor choices. We choose to remember a little hurt or misunderstanding, little slights that were probably unintended—and even if there wasn't the best motive in the world behind them, they are still such little things. We foolishly choose to remember and remember these things. By the very remembering, we give them a growth to which they have no right. In horticulture, there are many entrepreneurs today who try to force growth. They try to make an orange much bigger than an orange has any right to be; and in order to force fruits or flowers to be bigger, they do wrong things to them. In the same way, by choosing to remember and remember the little sufferings of life, we are making them much bigger than they have any right to be. They become freaks in our spiritual life, and a freak is a very frightening phenomenon.

In the other direction, we can ask ourselves: How often do I choose to remember the smallest kindness that was done to me? How often do I remember the smiles that were given to me, when I know in my heart that I wasn't deserving of any? Maybe my behavior on a particular day was not something to elicit smiles from my sisters, but I received a lot of smiles anyway. Do I remember that? Do I remember all the times I have been forgiven? How many times in my life have I received the Sacrament of Penance? It would be a good activity for us to engage in: to have a grateful memory for every absolution we have received, every forgiveness we have received, every forgiving smile we received from someone.

Abraham could have remembered all the wrong things: "I have to go to a strange land." "God has contradicted himself. It will never work out." But we know he chose to remember that God had said, "Your descendants will be more numerous than the stars in the heavens and the sands of the seashore." It was not without a struggle that he remembered these things.

We look at ourselves with a marveling smile and a shake of the head as we recognize our tendency to remember the things that make us miserable and to forget so easily the things that make us happy. For our encouragement, we can see ourselves in the apostles, who made some choices of memory that weren't all that good, but became better, and then became great—so that they became martyrs. At first, they didn't much care to remember what our Lord had said: "Unless you turn and become like children, you will never enter the kingdom of heaven" (Mt 18:3). They were squabbling about who was going to be first in the Kingdom of heaven when our Lord told them with such penetrating gentleness (which is more devastating than any hard, loud word), "First? Who will be first? If you're not like a little child, you won't even get in, so you don't need to worry about who's going to be first —you won't be there at all!" (see Mk 9:33–37). For a while, it seemed that they didn't much care to remember that, because they got into the same difficulties again.

Our Lord told them that he would be buffeted, spat

upon, ridiculed, murdered. It's obvious that they wanted to pretend he never said this. Because they did not choose to remember what he said, there was a penalty, so to speak —they also did not remember he had said that he would rise on the third day (see Mt 16:21). We must not penalize ourselves in that way. If we do not remember the stringency of the spiritual life which God has put plainly before us—that we must take up our cross each day and follow him—then we cannot even be called a disciple. Not to remember these things is to make ourselves like the apostles, who saw the empty tomb and did not know what had happened. They could not make the connection because they didn't remember what he had said. Our penalty will be the inability to remember that he has also said that he will triumph; that his will shall be done; that with him, nothing is impossible. We forget so easily that with God all things are possible, and nothing is impossible with God. How often do we choose to remember that? Instead, we choose to say, "I can't do it. It's beyond me. It won't work out. It's not possible. It won't be different. I can't get the better of this problem in my life. I can't overcome this." And so on. We don't remember his power; we don't remember his love.

It would be good to search the Scriptures, beginning with the Old Testament, for expressions of remembering. In Exodus, Moses tells God: "Remember Abraham! Remember your promises to him. Remember Isaac and your promises to him, and remember Jacob and your promises to him. It's not good for you to think about us right now at the present moment!" God seemed to enjoy this. God changed his mind. He relented from the punishment he was to give, because Moses sought to "refresh God's memory", as it were (see Ex 32:13, 14). In our own lives, too, we must "remind" God often that he said, "For with God nothing will be impossible" (Lk 1:37).

We determine the caliber of our spiritual life by what we choose to remember and what we choose to forget. By repeated acts of forgetting what is not worth remembering, we can come to the point where we recognize some things as not even worth the effort of forgetting. This is the peak. They simply cease to be within our memory, as it were, because the memory has been repeatedly filled with what is worth remembering.

Let us remember that each one of us is completely in charge of her own memory. When things are thrown on the screen of memory by the imagination, we are still in charge, because we can choose not to remember these things. Let me repeat the questions I asked before: Why are we so foolish as to choose to remember the things that make us miserable? Why do we often choose to remember the things that abort our growth? Why do we often choose to remember things that darken our mind and understanding, so that we do not see the spiritual meaning of situations, circumstances, happenings, interventions of God? Why is it that often we don't even get as far as thinking of God at all, when we are caught up in thinking, "This isn't right, this circumstance is the problem", and so on? Why do we not remember how miserable we were when we indulged ourselves in wrongdoing of whatever kind? Why do we not remember how happy we were when we allowed God to achieve in us his victory of contrition, of truth, of humility, of love, of patience, of perseverance? There has never been a humble person who was unhappy while she was being humble. Let us be busy cultivating a good memory during these weeks of Lent.

MONDAY OF THE SECOND WEEK OF LENT

Being Heartily Sorry

Act of Contrition

O my God, I am heartily sorry for having offended you, and I hate and detest all my sins, because I dread the loss of heaven and the pains of hell; but most of all because they offend you, my God, who are all good and deserving of all my love. I firmly resolve, with the help of your grace, to confess my sins, to do penance, and to amend my life. Amen.

LAST WEEK WE CONSIDERED the Sacrament of Reconciliation. Let us now turn to a prayer that many of us have said since childhood: the "Act of Contrition". We begin by saying, "O my God, I am *heartily* sorry." Have we ever meditated enough on the tremendous meaning of that? A good confession is made not only from the mind, but from the heart as well. The heart does not always respond to the findings of the mind. The mind can consider, can conclude, but if there is to be a change in behavior, the heart must accept the findings of the mind. If the heart time and time again eludes or distorts or refuses to accept the findings of the mind, then the terrible consequence is that the mind itself becomes confused in its searchings and its findings until one could reach the most extreme outpost of untruth, when one's own mind no longer presents truth to oneself. This is the result of many rejections by the heart.

Then we say, "for having offended you", because the recognition in our life of one sin, one fault immediately widens the vision to see more of the whole. When the heart responds to the findings of the mind and says, "Yes, that is a poisonous weed that I have been nurturing", immediately that vision fans out, and we see more things. We do not say in this wonderful formula that we are sorry for these sins of the past two weeks, but that we are sorry for having offended God. Then we say to him, "I hate and detest all my sins." If we listen carefully, we will surely hear God saying in our hearts, "I hate them, too." Something that can lead us away from the hatred of sin is a hatred of ourselves. No matter what we have done, no matter how we have erred, God never hates *us*. We delude ourselves in thinking that self-hatred is an expression of contrition. I hate my sins, not myself.

Then, I go forward and admit to God in a wonderfully honest, childlike way that I do not wish to go to hell, I do not wish to be condemned. I know that I have merited this, but I want to see him. Then I tell him that I know he's all good, and that I am sorry, not so much because my report card this week is not so good, but because I have offended him and he deserves better than this. The focus is all on him: "You are all good and deserving of all my love." That is why I am sorry. That is why I want to do penance. If I have hurt someone, I am sorry not so much because I have behaved badly and perhaps this person thinks less of me, but I am sorry I have hurt the person. That is the purity of sorrow. It is not focused on myself; it is focused on the harm, the hurt I have inflicted on God, on his Church, on my family, on an individual.

Then we say what we are going to do: "I firmly resolve, with the help of your grace, to confess my sins." There are no two ways about this; it is going to be a purposeful thing, a determined thing, a resolute thing. We do not say, "I am really going to try to do better." We say, "I firmly resolve." But from my own resources this resolve is not going to reach very far, because I am weak, fallible, prone to sin and fault. We cannot do anything without the help of his grace.

The "Act of Contrition" shows us what is basically wrong with giving general absolution in penitential services without serious necessity, such as the danger of death: it keeps us from individual confession of sins. As Pope Saint John Paul II said some years ago, "We have no right to deprive anyone of this personal encounter with Christ." It is a personal encounter with Christ to confess my sins and then to do penance.

There is a story I love about Saint Benedict Joseph Labre, recounting that he made a pilgrimage to Mount Alvernia where Saint Francis received the stigmata. The friars there saw him weeping and, supposing that he was a great sinner, expected to hear an appalling tale of the crimes he had committed. The young man on his knees before them confessed that he had never loved God enough, and they were stunned by this depth of purity.

Saint Benedict Joseph was right—this is the most terrible sin, and at the root of all sin. This great saint of God, who lived a most amazing life, who was truly without anything of his own, makes our little heads spin by his penances. He counted himself the greatest sinner and wept, "I have not loved God enough. I am the worst of all." This is the beautiful confession of someone who, growing in love of God, grew in a sense of sin. Let us see how we can deepen our sense of sin, our sense of faultiness, our sense of unworthiness, so that we can be happy.

Tuesday of the Second Week of Lent

A Sense of Opportunity

We recall how Pope Pius XII, many years ago, said so sadly, "What is the matter? This is the matter. The world has lost the sense of sin." Once we lose this sense of what must be changed in ourselves, then the spiritual life comes to a grinding halt.

Let us continue reviewing the "Act of Contrition". After we pray, "I firmly resolve, with the help of your grace, to confess my sins," we go on to the firm resolve without which the first expression would come to nothing: "to do penance, and to amend my life." Without God's enlightenment we would not see a need to do penance. We could be so utterly deluded as to think that perhaps there is nothing much to confess. Saint Clare says in her Testament, "The most high heavenly Father deigned through his mercy and grace to enlighten my heart that I should do penance." She who is so pure of heart, so holy, is happy to confide to us that she needed enlightenment. How much more do we!

The Latin expression for doing penance is *facere paenitentiam. Facere* is very broad in its usage; it is a very strong and creative word. It can be translated as "to do", but most basically *facere* means "to make". It is a word expressing not merely action, which could be imposed, but an act of creation. We would use this word for God's act of creation in making the world, in making man. This marvelous word means essentially "to build". It means also "to bring forth" or "to initiate". It means particularly "to cause to happen". When we speak in our own lives of *facere paenitentiam*, "to make penance", this is precisely what we mean: that we allow something to happen. Penitential occasions can arise every day, but it is up to us to allow them to happen.

Saint Clare tells us that God enlightened her heart so that she would do something positive with what she had, with what occurred, with what God provided, with what the day brought, with the conditions put before her. She says that Francis had observed in her little band of sisters that they "did not draw back from any deprivation, poverty, labor, trial, or scorn and contempt of the world, but rather that [they] reckoned them as great delights". They could not escape onerous burdens in life, nor could our Lord Jesus Christ, nor could our Lady, and neither can we. It is our decision whether we simply put up with things, try to get through them, or whether we make something wonderful of them. The sisters were making something wonderful of these difficulties, these onerous, painful things, and this is what made Saint Francis so happy. In the end, it was what made the sisters happy.

What I do with the difficult, burdensome, suffering situations in my life is a very personal decision: whether I lower my head and push through them, waiting for them to be over, whether I murmur about them, whether I try to get out of them, or whether I really exercise the power of *facere*, "to make". If we allow it, God enlightens our hearts to make penance, to make something beautiful out of these things, to make something conducive to growth in intimacy with our Lord Jesus.

The meaning of *facere* that I particularly love is, "to work in a particular direction so as to function successfully and usefully". Whether we make successful the sufferings and difficulties that are inevitable and unavoidable in human life is completely up to us. Often enough, do we not have to confess that instead of making penance, we waste it? Here are the opportunities, day after day, and perhaps we waste them. Do we not have to bow our heads in truthful contrition and say that sometimes our first reaction to something difficult, to something demanding is, "How do I get out of this? How can I escape from this? What excuse can I bring forward as to why I should not do this?" So we can waste, waste, waste, day after day, the opportunities to make penance, to make something beautiful, to make an act of self-abasement.

Paenitentia, too, is a most interesting word. What do we think of when we hear that word? The true meaning of the word is not a burden that we carry on our backs. *Paenitentia* means "an act of self-abasement". It is an act of regret for some wrong. Again, there can be a creative element. Each of us should desire to be an artist in her spiritual life, who does not just live with what is there, but who uses it to create something beautiful.

Would any one of us say, "I have no need to do penance, I have not done anything wrong, I have nothing to regret"? It makes us wince, and perhaps even smile ruefully, to think of it. A life as long as that of an Old Testament patriarch would not be sufficient to do penance for one venial sin. Yet we waste the opportunities so often.

There is never a real penitent who is not a joyous penitent. One who is dragging her feet, one who is trying to get out of suffering and escape sacrifice, is not a penitent at all. What we want to do as concerns penance is to develop a sense of "Here is my chance! Did I not promise myself, God, and my community in this 'Act of Contrition' that I resolve with the help of his grace to do penance? I have to keep my resolution. Here is God's answer!" We move, then, in this theology of the "Act of Contrition", from a sense of sin to a sense of opportunity.

I next promise to amend my life. Here again is a wonderful word: *emendo*. This means "to reform", to take my own life into my hands and shape it differently, as the potter shapes the clay. Here is something that is all out of line, here is something that is clumsy and unbeautiful; and I reform it, I reshape it, I set it right. Another meaning of *emendo* is "to remove defects". Many women in secular life will go to great lengths to remove defects from their face or from their figure. "For the children of this world are more prudent in dealing with their own generation than are the children of light" (Lk 16:8, NAB). How much effort do we make to remove defects, things that make us unbeautiful before God? A normal woman wants to be beautiful; and if she doesn't, there is something wrong with her. Shall a spiritual woman be less wise than the women of this world? Shall she not be eager to remove defects from her spirit, her soul, her heart?

Emendo also means "to cure a disease". Disease of the soul results from not making penance out of things sacrificial and suffering and of themselves onerous. Eventually this will lead to an even greater and fatal indolence, apathy, and malaise that says, "I am content to be sick. I don't want to get up. I don't want to get better. I am content to stay this way."

The final meaning of *emendo* is "to compensate, to bring something back" to God. This follows from *facere paenitentiam*. I have brought him many affronts, many disappointments. To amend my life means to bring him something else: something beautiful, something mended and repaired.

We go forward through the "Act of Contrition" in this firm resolve, knowing that we need God's grace, and happily knowing that this grace to make penance will never be refused. It has never happened that anyone came to God desiring to do penance with the help of his grace, and grace was withheld. God loves to enlighten us. God answers by saying, "This is just what I have been waiting to hear. You want some light on your situation. Here it is." He will never fail to enlighten us if we wish to be enlightened. But if we close our spiritual eyes, he will not force them open. He delights to enlighten. (I did not mean a play on words, but it is a lovely one.) He delights to enlighten us and will never refuse, will never delay. It is a bold prayer, because God will turn the light of truth upon what we really are, what we have really done, what we ought to do and must do, what we must amend, what we must repair and make beautiful.

Saint Clare says that the most high heavenly Father enlightened her heart. She is speaking here of her first turning, her entering upon the way of Francis. This is only the first conversion. After her first conversion, he enlightened her that there was more and more to do and to amend. Every conversion in our lives calls us to the next conversion. There is never a point, a day, an hour in life when I can sit back and say, "I am converted!" Yes, I have made a turn, but it invites me to make yet another turn, which calls me to a deeper conversion, to a conversion I would not have been able to see until I made this one. Thus the enlightenment goes on also. If it may be said rightly that one unrepented sin leads to another, it is also happily true that one conversion leads to another. Let us be occupied in praying for enlightenment and using that enlightenment to become determined, with God's grace, not to waste opportunities for penance, but to make them something beautiful, something availing, something serving my own relationship with Jesus, and something that furthers the progress of the Church on earth.

Wednesday of the Second Week of Lent

True Greatness

In today's Gospel Jesus asked the apostles, "Are you able to drink the chalice that I am going to drink?" (Mt 20:22). "We can!" was the ready answer; but how quickly they found out that they could not. We can see our poor selves in the apostles as they all declared firmly that they could do anything, as they showed that they found the idea of sitting on thrones very inviting and quite agreeable, as they insisted that they would never leave him. In one of the saddest sentences in all Scripture, we read, "Then all the disciples deserted him and fled" (Mt 26:56). They left him alone when he needed them most, yet his love was persistent. Although they ran away from all he had taught them, his love brought them back. It is not so much that love simply calls; love also brings back. Love is always reclaiming. What a reclaiming was theirs: to be loved into martyrdom. They were to be much greater than they ever could have dreamed in their first worldly ambitions. Even in their most extravagant musings on their own greatness, not one of them had ever touched on the idea that they were called to be saints and martyrs, "witnesses" to him who is all love, to him who is all humility.

The petty ambition displayed in today's Gospel turns up again at that sacred moment when Christ gave us the chalice of his own blood to drink. In this sad scene of noticeably human persons bickering over who was the greatest, we find a God whose love was and is indefatigable, whose incredible humility showed its durability beyond human understanding; and out of this setting, he led a community, singing. They went out together, singing a psalm (see Mt 26:30). They were to make more mistakes in the future, but ultimately they would come out singing, all because of Jesus' love, humility, and unflagging faith in them. His faith in them was so great that he even tried, until the last moment, to save his betrayer through love: he called him "friend".

At the Last Supper Jesus taught us what community is. The Church which he founded was to be a community. Jesus was a community person. He was not a solitary. When, for short intervals, he went off alone to pray to his Father, it was not only in order to gather strength for his own humanity, it was also always for the sake of the apostles. He always came back to them from his Father, renewed in strength. Even when he ascended to the Father, it was "to go and prepare a place" for them, for his community.

This is what he teaches us about the founding of his Church. Once his love and humility have empowered the poverty of our limited human understanding, our mistakes, and our blundering, then out of such poverty can come something that is singing, something that becomes, indeed, a witness. The Church must be founded in the heart of each of us. Our Lord's love and humility can make something enduring and strong out of our poverty, if only we will allow him.

The first Pope protested about what Jesus was to do at that Last Supper; then he quickly withdrew his protest when faced with the alternative of not being with Jesus. Often we protest in our hearts at things we do not understand; we say, "No, this can't be!" But let us pray for one another, that we will withdraw our protests as quickly as Peter did, when we receive that glimmer of understanding which enables us to see that "if this is not to be"—whatever he asks of us in life—then we "will have no part with him." After all, the only tragedy is not to be with him.

Through all the centuries, Jesus has been calling community together. He who is the second Person of the community of Father, Son, and Holy Spirit is always building community; and we are never more his than when we are building community, understanding that it is built, not with brilliance or illustriousness or anything the world may recognize as great, but with love and humility. Just as he led his little band that night, may he lead us out of our mistakes, our limitations, our poverty—singing a song of community. His love was so great that he simply would not allow it to be overcome by what might seem to us the most overwhelming evidence that he was mistaken and that they could not do that to which he was beckoning them, which they themselves did not even understand. Out of his faith in his own, out of his enduring love for this small band of persons, came his Church. Out of us also can come his Church if we will help him in his work of founding a new and enduring Church in each other, if we will allow him and help him to love us into holiness, to love us into martyrdom. The heart has many martyrdoms, and his love calls us to sustain them all.

Thursday of the Second Week of Lent

A Change of Heart

In Lent, the Church challenges us to a change of heart and encourages us by telling us that Lent is for scoundrels. She doesn't say, "Come, all my holy ones, and change your hearts even more." She doesn't say, "Come, all of my perfect ones." But she says in the most realistic words that any mother could ever use, "Let the scoundrel forsake his way, and the wicked man his thoughts; let him turn to the Lord for mercy; to our God, who is generous in forgiving" (Is 55:7, NAB).

We don't enter into Lent as though this season is for all the good people who are going to become better, and so if I am going to get into this assembly I will have to sneak in by some back door. But the more I am aware of my need of redemption, the more do I enter the portals of Lent as the scoundrel I am, knowing that this is why Lent is given to us.

The Church says realistically, "Come on, scoundrels, let's see what we can do about becoming holy." She calls these very scoundrels to heights of holiness, to a change of heart, to a change of spirit. She brings us a sense of spaciousness, of largeness. Scripture says, "As the heavens are higher than the earth, so are my ways higher than your ways and my thoughts than your thoughts" (Is 55:9). If we remain earthbound, we shall never begin to understand the ways of God. If we have only an earthly prudence, an earthly concern for ourselves, a human psychology and sociology, and the valuable findings of natural anthropology, then we shall never, never have the largeness of spirit which is essential for a change of heart. Our thoughts may be perfectly organized sociologically, psychologically, anthropologically, anthropomorphically, and so on down the list of impressive and meaningful words, but they shall never be the thoughts of God, because our thoughts are only human things. They are only tools that can help us toward the great change of heart that the Church asks.

We can examine this concept of change through the paradox that it is only out of something that is changeless, something that is really immutable, that we are able to change. Real change comes from changelessness. In today's First Reading and Responsorial Psalm we have that very beautiful and familiar image of the tree that is planted by the living waters (see Jer 17:8, Ps 1:3). Exegetes have usually understood the waters as a symbol for God. The Church puts down its roots so deep that when everything gets hot and sultry, the tree can still remain green. But that is not to say that this tree doesn't have a winter, that it doesn't have an autumn, that there isn't a time when its leaves drop to the ground. The Scriptures are telling us that the tree is always living because its roots are put down near the running waters of God and draw sustenance from God. In this sense the tree is changeless whether it drops its leaves or puts out its leaves season upon season, whether it is lush in summer, dried and seared in late summer, bare in the winter, glorious in the springtime. There is something changeless about it because this symbolic tree is rooted in God, and so it can sway with the breezes. It can blossom, it can grow bare, it can survive all these seasons. Unless we are put down into the changelessness of God, we can never have a *metanoia*.

After Vatican Council II, we were called upon to examine the structures of religious life and of the entire Church, and this continues even now. There is a great movement in our era against anything that is stereotyped. This is very good, for there is much that we have allowed to become stereotyped. However, we need to have deep roots, and we need to do some very clear thinking to be able to separate what is stereotyped in itself and what is stereotyped in us. We are given the changeless words of Scripture, and it all depends on the reader whether they are vital to one's life, whether one is changed by them. It would be a very shallow conclusion to say, "Let's write a new Gospel, because we have been reading these over and over year after year and we know them by heart and are getting tired of them." While we would scarcely say this of the Scriptures, we can sometimes say this much too quickly of the helpful ceremonies of the Church, the helpful settings of our own lives, or our relations with one another.

Change cannot be forced. If you take someone and push him from one room to another, he is physically in the other room, but for all real purposes he is right back in the room where he wanted to be. This is why a change of heart must be wished and willed. Holiness must be wanted, must be sought. Change must be evaluated, and then it must be accepted and developed with willingness and with understanding. There is nobody more unchanged than a person on whom change has been forced. There is no heart so unchanged as one on which ascetical practices have been imposed, because this heart will not be liberated but enchained. What we want to do is to inspire one another's hearts, open one another's hearts, not by sitting over them with a crowbar, but by allowing each one to be her true self.

Cardinal Merry del Val talks about sanctifying the prose of daily life. I would like to enlarge that and say that we want to transpose the prose of daily life into the poetry of love. This is up to each one to do. There are many ways of sweeping a hall. Some ways are creative, some are not. There are many ways of drying the dishes. Some are beautiful and womanly; some are crude and unlovely. With everything we do, spontaneity comes from the heart. So we favor spontaneity, we favor change, we favor anything that is real, and we can establish these things only out of the unchangeable.

Friday of the Second Week of Lent

Redeeming One Another

We want to be more deeply united with Christ in his Passion. There is no doubt about that. Everyone here wants this. But we know that often enough we need to hang our poor heads in shame, because we do indeed want to be deeply united with the redemptive Christ but without any cost of suffering to ourselves. It sounds brutal when we put it that way, but cleansing truth often has a good brutality about it, brutality in the sense that it brings us up short. It deals us a blow that we badly need. We want to face these realities in ourselves. Suffering always surprises us in our lives because we don't want to suffer. We don't know how to deal with it, and that is why Christ our Lord has shown us how to deal with it.

One can say, although the words sound shocking, that in the profoundest sense suffering has no meaning of itself. People who want to suffer for the sake of suffering are mentally disturbed. This is not normal, nor is it human. Christ willed his sufferings because they were for us, not because he liked to suffer, not because he liked to see his blood flow, not because he liked to be wounded, not because he liked to be rejected, not because he liked to be scorned. His suffering was part of a deeper mystery.

In Lent we enter into a new understanding of the mystery of the suffering of Christ. It is a great mystery. Why did he will to do it this way? Obviously to penetrate our dullness with an understanding of how much we are loved. We cannot look at a crucifix without being moved, and we understand something of his love when we see the Son of God enduring the untold physical sufferings of the Passion and the crucifixion. Rejection is a very hard thing to suffer—being rejected by those whom he loved, by those whom he had come to save. He suffered all his life by being mocked and jeered at by some, by being repudiated, by having his love thrown back in his face. Lent is a profound season in which we want to ponder deeply these mysteries of his redemptive love.

Our redemption was wrought by the Son of God, the Redeemer. What is a redeemer? A redeemer is a purchaser. When we redeem something, we buy it back. If an item has been offered in pawn so that the owner can get some immediate monetary help, someone else can come and redeem it. The person who does this has to pay a price. We are continuing the redeeming work of the Son. We are called to be co-redeemers of one another, to fill up what is wanting in the sufferings of Christ. This buying back of one another for Christ is supposed to cost something. This is obvious, but like all evident truths it can elude us so easily. It is part of our fallen nature that we have a certain knack for complexities but the simple truth we can quite miss, just like a person who walks into a door and says, "It wasn't closed yesterday." When we speak of redeeming others, we don't mean that we set out rubbing our hands enthusiastically to cure everybody of the faults that we see in them. If we love this idea of redeeming one another back from weakness and faults, we have to pay something for this. If we are redeeming the impatient person, we do this at cost to our own patience. If we are trying to redeem and buy back the weak person for Christ, we do this at the cost of our tolerance, in the best sense of that word: bearing her up by our effort, our self-discipline.

Let us be perfectly clear what we mean by redeeming one another. By buying back a loved one for Christ, we buy her back to her original image in the mind of God, which is all-beautiful, and lovely to behold. Thus, redemption means helping another to be the beautiful, unique, blessed person she is. The faults take care of themselves. There is all the difference in the world between helping someone to overcome her faults and helping someone want to be her best self.

We shouldn't be surprised that it costs us something to redeem another. We were bought at a great price, as we say again and again in the liturgy (1 Cor 6:20, 1 Pet 1:18–19). If we were bought at a great price, we should realize that others are also bought at a great price. We should be willing to empty out the pockets of our energy, our love, our forgiveness, our compassion to buy them back so that each one may want to have a change of heart and so that no one ever has to be cajoled, pushed, or pulled into holiness. Because of our love and understanding and acceptance, each person is enabled to take to herself the abundant grace of this season, and to find springing up within herself a great thirst for holiness.

Saturday of the Second Week of Lent

The Prodigal Son

Today's Gospel presents the parable of the Prodigal Son, where we see the two sons of the father, seeming so disparate and yet having their sin in common: that they were all for themselves and not for the father (see Lk 15:11–32). The younger son wanted all his inheritance and his money for himself. The other son really wanted the same thing, only he went about it in a different way, his self-righteous way. The younger son said, "Give me the inheritance", which he certainly did not deserve. The elder son thought he was living in such a way that he was deserving of all the wealth. So we have here two unloving sons.

The younger son says, "Give me the share of the estate that is coming to me." What he really meant was, "Why aren't you dead so I can have my inheritance? Since you won't do me the favor of dying so I can have my inheritance, give it to me now." It's horrible, isn't it? There is no limit to the cruelty of a person turned in upon himself: "I want what I want."

We know what this son went through. The father did

give his inheritance to him, and he wasted all of it. He lived a dissolute, sinful life. The father, in a sense, punished him by giving him what he asked. What we demand in selfishness and manage to get—"I want it my way, and I want it right now"—can be God's penalty. He says, "All right, here it is. Take it." Then we, in our own way, come to the same end as this younger son. We want it, we want it now, but it all goes sour, and it is all dissipated.

Finally the son did come to his senses, and this tells us that we should never despair because of our faults. Sometimes we have to fall very low before coming to our senses. It was a great grace that he came to his senses. But in the beginning it wasn't for a very lofty reason. He was hungry, and he wished he could have the same lunch the pigs were having, he who had feasted in the house of his father. So he did come to his senses enough to think: "How many hired hands in my father's house are surrounded with opulence compared to what I have—nothing?" But the accent is still on himself.

As we see in the parable, God is so humble that he accepts even such non-lofty intentions. The son came back all bedraggled, remembering that things were much better before he acted in this fashion. He hadn't come nearly so far as pure contrition, that perfect act of contrition. We know the technical difference between perfect contrition and imperfect contrition: it is perfect when it is motivated by love of God and imperfect if it rests on other motives, such as fear of punishment. God doesn't say, "I accept only perfect contrition", but God accepts imperfect contrition, which was all the son had at the time. It was quite notably imperfect.

On the way the son was rehearsing what he would say: "Father, I have sinned against heaven and against you." Now he had come to a point beyond his own hunger, his own need, his own misery. He realized that he had offended God by hurting his father. Another big step forward came when he said, "I don't deserve to be called your son." He realized he had no right to be called a son: "Treat me as a hired hand." This was his highest ambition, to be a servant.

The son was "still a long way off". It wasn't only that the father was watching at the window, or at the door, but he was peering, squinting his eyes for the least sign of him on the horizon. When he was still a long way off, the father caught sight of him, and the text says, "He ran out to meet him, threw his arms around his neck and kissed him." He must not have looked very kissable, and he surely didn't appear very huggable. Sometimes in our relations with others we want to wait around until they look a little more kissable and their behavior is a little more huggable. But this is not what the father did. After he had squinted down that road, he ran and he kissed him just the way he was. He didn't wait until his wounds were cleansed and he was washed up, but kissed him right then and there.

The son made his little speech. The father didn't just

call his servants and say, "Somebody do this, and somebody do that." His first word was "Quick!" That was the whole first sentence. He couldn't wait to reinstate him, and this was what must have humbled the son to the dust. When we have realized the heinousness of our sins and have been brought to contrition by forgiveness, we would be grateful to hear, "All right, you do penance now for seven years and then come back." But the father says, "Quick! Bring out the finest robe. Put it on him. Put a ring on his finger; put shoes on his feet."

Then we have the elder son whose basic sin is just the same. He wanted it all for himself, except that he was going to arrive at the inheritance not in a demanding way, but perhaps in a more self-righteous way: "I am so upright. It is all coming to me. It all belongs to me." He grew angry. And then what did the father do? Sometimes it is much harder to deal with a self-righteous person than with a gross sinner, but the father goes out to him, too. The elder son wouldn't come in. The father could have said, "Let him stay out there." From what you see of him in this parable, it would have been a much happier party without him. But the father goes out after him, too. It's hard to plead with a self-righteous person. It's easier to plead with a profligate. Then the elder son said the terrible word that showed that he apparently never loved the father, "I have *slaved* for you." One would never say such a word to a person one loved. He didn't say, "Don't you love me? I have tried to be faithful." But no, "I have slaved for you." It showed what his relationship was with the father. "I have worked like a slave; hand over what is coming to me." A terrible thing. Again, the father didn't say, "How dare you speak to me like that! It's clear you don't love me!" Instead, he called this self-righteous person "my son". But this son was so in love with his own righteousness that he didn't know how to celebrate.

We find sinners in the New Testament who did know how to celebrate. Levi, who was to become Saint Matthew, threw a party for our Lord and all the local riffraff came. He was a sinner, but he knew how to celebrate because he knew how to be forgiven. The elder son didn't think there was any need for forgiveness. He was out there slaving, always doing what was right, and not in need of forgiveness. God's punishment was that he didn't know how to celebrate. It is when we realize that we are sinners, that we have no right to anything, and that God still forgives us, that we know how to celebrate. We are not depressed, we are not discouraged, but we are contrite, which is a very different thing.

I think we must take this Gospel phrase by phrase and never imagine we completely understand it, for we can always deepen our sense of what contrition is, what forgiveness is. God never wants to give up. God is giving us that figure of himself in the father. It is almost unbelievable. He is the one who waits and waits for the profligate son to return. He is the one who goes out to his elder son, this odious, self-righteous person. Welcoming his younger son, the father celebrates even a good intention that has not yet reached a peak of nobility. But (and I say it with all possible reverence) God is ready to celebrate for almost no reason at all. Just the smallest sign of conversion and God is ready to celebrate. Shall we do less?

THIRD WEEK OF LENT

Third Sunday of Lent, Year A

Coming Alive

In the liturgy of the third Sunday of Lent, the First Reading at Holy Mass describes the Israelites in whom we so clearly recognize our miserable little selves, who are given everything and are complaining and grumbling. Then they receive another gift of God and complain some more. They want water and they tell God so. Then God shows his great power, and a great miracle takes place (see Ex 17:3–7). Striking a rock is an unlikely way to find water!

In the Gospel we read more about water. The incident with the Samaritan woman moves my heart so deeply. It is so rich. It is one of the longest Gospel readings the Church gives us at Holy Mass. I would ask you to take it sentence by sentence in your prayer (see Jn 4:5–42).

First of all, our dear Lord is tired. This is such an endearing revelation of his humanity. He had been walking; he had been preaching; he had been correcting the apostles, sometimes receiving from them a good response and sometimes finding in them a depressing (humanly speaking) lack of understanding. He is tired and he sits down. When we experience our small fatigues, and small indeed they are, we can unite them with his, knowing he was also tired.

Then he begins to speak to this woman. He knows everything about her, just as he knows everything about every one of us. Her faults are great. Her sins are flagrant. How does he approach her? Does he, so to speak, curl his lip? Does he draw back, does he show aversion? No, and he knows all about her. In what we might want to call an arch manner, he invites her to make a good confession, which she doesn't do at first. No one can be forced into the truth about herself, but she can be invited with love.

He asks for a drink, and this too is so moving. This is not a fiction. He is really thirsty and he would like a drink, and he asks her. He doesn't think, "She is beneath my notice. I'll get a drink somewhere else." Then she questions him. In response he says, "If you but recognized the gift of God." How often, we wonder, does our dear Lord have to say this to us, day in and day out? Each Lenten day he is reaching out gifts to us. How many gifts has he reached out today? There has been the supreme gift of himself in Holy Communion; but how many little portions of grace have gone unrecognized? How many times have we driven Jesus to say, "If you only recognized the gift of God"? No one would be such an utter fool as to throw a gift away, yet we are just that foolish sometimes.

We know how this conversation unfolds. He invites her to penitence. This Stranger sits down and makes this very peculiar request of her, a Samaritan, although Jews don't talk to Samaritans. He says, "Go and get your husband", as if to say, "I'd like to talk to the two of you." Then we have her response. Reaching blindly for the truth, even in her faltering effort to cover up, she says, "I have no husband." Does he look at her with blame? I think he must have smiled at her a little. "You're right. You have had five. This one is not your husband." We don't find her desperate. We find her already on the way to healing because she recognizes the love in this. He is not saying the equivalent of, "You no-good woman, you have had one man after another." He says, "Yes, that's right, he's not your husband."

So her heart opens, as every heart opens to love. She did not then justify herself. There must have been more to this conversation, because she later tells the townsfolk, "Come and hear this man. He has told me everything I ever did." I imagine there was quite a bit more that he told her. But she did not need to justify herself because she knew she was loved and he had invited her to confess, not tried to overwhelm her with his power. She had some intimation that he was not an ordinary person. Did she perhaps have some inkling in her heart that this was the Messiah? She says, "I know that the Messiah is coming, the one called the Anointed; when he comes, he will tell us everything." Is she not revealing that she suspects this is the Messiah? Otherwise why would she say this? It doesn't follow on the conversation as concerns literary progression. I wonder if she didn't tilt her head a little and look at him, perhaps half closing her eyes as she said this.

He responds in that utterly overwhelming sentence—it is so short: "I who speak to you am he." This dear, dear Lord of ours is often—to our stilted way of thinking, our unpredictable Lord—is telling this sinful woman who he is. How many times does he silence the devils? He silences other people: "Don't say I am the Messiah." But to her who has responded to his love, who is looking at him and who makes this statement that must have drifted off into silence, "I know a Messiah is coming . . .", he says grandly, "I am he." He says this to her (of all people, we might say): "I who am speaking to you am he."

And to us, too, it is he who is speaking throughout the day. He is calling. I will tell you something extremely intimate. I was just lost in the wonder of this Gospel, and it struck me, looking at the Sacred Host, that he is saying this to me. He is saying this to each one of us: "I who look at you am he." Perhaps this would be a help to you in your prayer. It has been an immense help to me. It was a tremendous grace, and I cannot keep any grace for myself. "I who look at you am he."

He called this woman by his love to repent, and that is what made her free, so that she didn't care anymore if everyone in the world knew all of her sins. Off she went and said, "Come see a man who told me everything I have done. Could he possibly be the Messiah?" Maybe she was inviting the townsfolk to the first public penance service. They came because they must have been overcome by this woman whose way of life was rather well known, but who was so happy that this stranger knew all about her. Who was he? They did come and they did listen and they made him stay. They prevailed on him to remain with them: "Tell us some more." One cannot doubt that he told them some things about themselves, because afterward they say, "Now we believe not because of what you say, but because of what we've heard ourselves." They too were made free by the truth.

I can hardly say more. It is one of the most powerful and tender passages in all of the Scriptures. He is asking us questions, too, and inviting us to repentance. We want to come more alive now in this next week of Lent. Certainly this woman came alive out of a morass of sin. She must have danced through that city. The Gospel says she went into the town: "Listen to this! Come and hear it yourselves." When we are aware of our own sins and of the fact that we have been forgiven, then love always runs out to others. We can never keep mercy to ourselves. His mercy makes demands. According as we know we have been forgiven, so must we be forgiving. According as we know mercy has been poured out upon us, the more there is the absolute demand to love others.

This is perhaps one of the clearest pictures of Jesus we are given in any of the Gospels: how he deals with sinners, how patient he is in drawing good from us, how mindful of our weakness he is. He never knocks us down or treads upon us. He is always trying to evoke and invite the truth from us. He always reveals himself in some measure when we respond to the truth about ourselves, even though, like the woman, we have little tricks that keep us from going down to the root of our sins. She went dancing back into that city one happy woman. She had really gotten to the bottom of things. Then we see the reward: he is able to reveal himself and to make us understand that, "I who speak to you, I am he. I who give you this opportunity, I am he. I who call out to you, I am he. I who am looking at you, I am he."

Third Sunday of Lent, Year B

The Right Kind of Zeal

In today's Gospel, the disciples see Jesus cleansing the temple of merchants, and they apply to him these words of Scripture: "Zeal for your house has consumed me" (Ps 69:9). When we want to know if our ardor is Christ's zeal or our own self-serving zeal, then let us see who is being consumed. The false and bitter zeal that eats up other persons is not the zeal of Christ. Real zeal consumes *me*. This is the zeal of Christ. Saint Francis died of zeal. Zeal for God's house had eaten him up quite literally. He was burned out. Saint Clare died of zeal: her zeal for penitence had wasted her body. May it be that we die of zeal. It is such a wonderful thing to be worn out, to be used up for God. What else would we ever want to do with our lives? This has nothing to do with emotion. Emotional verve can be a good servant, but it is a poor leader. Why? Because it is not dependable, and leadership must be dependable. Emotional verve comes and goes. It is certainly not to be despised. It is very beautiful. It is a great aid, but it is not that on which we can depend. Sometimes when we would like to feel élan, it is notably absent. Sometimes when we could perhaps do with a little less of it, it is too present, a bit too obtrusive.

And so zeal, which by definition is "ardent enthusiasm", is a matter of the will. Our dear Lord was not zealous in an emotional sense for his agony in the Garden. He would have been an anomaly of humanity if he had been. He was not emotionally zealous to be crucified, to be given ingratitude often enough for his favors. But he had zeal of the will, and that is what real zeal is. When we pray to serve God with greater zeal, we pray that we will be more directed to do his will.

Zeal is never static, nor does it ever reach what one might call its high level and abide there. Zeal is dynamic; if it is not greater all the time, it is not zeal. Each day it should eat up more of us, so that there is less and less of us. We can cry out with Saint John the Baptist, "I must decrease" (Jn 3:30). The most wonderful grace is that he may increase, that I give him more and more room to grow in me. Zeal has to be greater all the time. This is the immediate reward of real zeal, that it is always pushing on. It is contemplative action. Zeal could never say, "Well, that's enough now, I have it and I'm really a zealous person. I feel great zeal." There must always be more giving, more loving, more compassion, until I am consumed. Hopefully I can say at my death as Saint Paul said, "It is no longer I who live, but Christ who lives in me" (Gal 2:20).

❦

Third Sunday of Lent, Year C

Assimilation

In today's First Reading from Exodus, Moses is growing more and more nervous about the difficult mission God is giving to him, and he asks what credentials he should take. God replies: "This is what you shall tell the Israelites: I am sent me to you" (Ex 3:14, NAB). It is I am who sends us into the challenges of each day. It is I am who through the voice of conscience tells us what to do, and yet we must make our own decisions.

This is pointed out very clearly in the Second Reading from Corinthians. I am sent Moses to Pharaoh, but Pharaoh chose not to listen. In the Letter to the Corinthians we are reminded that in the desert the Israelites all ate the same food: the miraculous food, the prefigurement of the Blessed Sacrament. They all drank miraculously from the same struck rock. But Scripture says that God was not pleased with most of them, because they grumbled and did not spiritually assimilate the food or allow themselves to be spiritually renewed and refreshed by the drink (see 1 Cor 10:1–6).

We eat the Food of the Eucharist, we all drink the Precious Blood. Why are not all the results the same?

What keeps us from assimilating this heavenly Food? What keeps our spiritual thirst from being slaked by the Precious Blood? What do we grumble about? Are we preoccupied with small angers, little resentments, little troubles about work, little complaints, indulged ambitions to measure my worth by outer success, even though it is inner success that counts for anything with God? God leads us into this new week of Lent reminding us that we are eating of the Bread of Life more truly than our forefathers in the desert who ate the manna, indeed miraculous, but such a small figure of that on which we are being fed. We can excuse them for being given so much and bringing so little return, because we know that God himself is given to us, and sometimes we bring him very little return.

We are told in the Gospel about that fig tree and about another chance. The master is very displeased: "Where are the figs?" Then this figure of the servant becomes the figure of Christ, the Son, who is speaking to the Father, "Let me try again. Let me do this and this and this to it." What is the "this and this and this" for us? It is the graces of Lent given to us: the little penances, the little offerings, the little silencings of the heart. God has given us another Lent. Jesus has said to the Father, "Leave this fig tree another year, and I will try again" (see Lk 13:1–9).

Let us take this parable deeply into our hearts, and let us take these readings into our hearts. It is I AM who has called me; it is I AM, the all-powerful One, who gives me the power to live this Lent as he desires. I have nothing to worry about and I have no excuse, because I am someone who was made by I AM. I was called by I AM. I am to do what I am asked to do by I AM.

As we are fed with the Bread of Life and drink from the Rock that is Christ himself, may God be able to say that he is pleased, because we understand better and we are so grateful to have another week of Lent. Leave it another Lent, our suffering Savior has said, and let me try. He is trying. It remains with us whether I AM will be successful. I AM was not successful with Pharaoh. I AM will be successful with us insofar as we allow him. So let us truly assimilate our heavenly Food as never before. Let our thirst be truly slaked by that Precious Blood, knowing that we belong to I AM, who is all-powerful and who gives us this all-sustaining Food. There is nothing that one who has received the Holy Eucharist is not able to do.

Monday of the Third Week of Lent

Dying and Rising

LENT IS A SEASON OF PENANCE, yes, but it is also a season of many, many resurrections preparing us for *the* Resurrection. Each of us is a little Lazarus, called by every moment of grace to come forth, to rise from the death-like quality of our persistent faults. Our dear Lord in his humanity was rising all of his life. He was rising out of many deaths before the great Resurrection. Let us look together at some of these risings during his human life.

Some of them were almost incredible, such as the time when his townsmen wanted to throw him over the brow of the hill (see Lk 4:24–30). From the fall of Adam and Eve there has been the tendency in human nature to be envious, to be jealous, to be unwilling to accept the greatness of others for fear it would diminish oneself. But it is not a very frequent thing that your fellow townspeople should want to throw you over the brow of the hill. Since Jesus was perfectly human, he felt this more deeply than any of us ever could. He was rejected by his own townspeople, whom he had come to save. He rose out of this. He simply passed through their midst. I think we can truly say he used his divine power to pass through their midst with a very aching human heart. He had to make an effort to rise. We want to reject all of those spiritual enemies that want to throw us from the brow of the hill. We want to be like our Jesus in that we rise again, we leave the field of temptation and rise in his victory.

Then he certainly had to rise out of his seeming failures, even with his own. Many accepted him, and many didn't. One of his very own—Judas—betrayed him. Can we begin to fathom the depth of Jesus' suffering to have one of his own loved group betray him, reject him? He rose out of that. He didn't dissolve his little community. He didn't leave them, but he rose out of this betrayal. Only when we ponder that can we understand the agony of his heart. We see him rise up and go forward.

Then there was dear Philip, who still seemed so obtuse after several years of instruction from the greatest of all teachers, the God-Man. We can almost hear the sigh of Jesus when we read, "Have I been with you so long, and yet you do not know me, Philip?" (Jn 14:9). It was a tired but loving sigh. Surely he must often say in our hearts this word, "So many times have I told you this; so long have I been with you and you still don't understand?" Jesus knew that eventually Philip would understand, and so he waited. But it was something out of which he had to rise.

At the Last Supper he said, "It is you who have stood by me in my trials" (Lk 22:28, NAB). We read the Scriptures and wonder, "When was that?" They always seemed to be notably non-present when there was something to be suffered or when there was something to be understood. But he was looking forward to what they could be. The timeless God said, "You are the ones who have stood by me." I think even they, who were always ready for a compliment, must have been stopped by that. Maybe they shifted around a little bit. What he said was a prophecy. He looked beyond what they were, to what they could be through his unflagging love and humility. Let us remember that his love did not endure without the cost of pain, for he was perfectly human. One day his saying that they stood by him in trials would be fulfilled unto martyrdom.

Then Jesus rose out of the hurt caused by his own beloved three, the three he took intimately into the heart of his agony in the Garden. He found them asleep. He knew they were weak, as he knows we are weak. Yet it hurt him so much. How would we feel if physically we were suffering very much, and someone who was staying with us fell asleep out of weakness? He was hurt, and we know this because he said, "So could you not watch with me one hour?" (Mt 26:40). Then he rose up and verified his belief in these weak men on whom he built his Church, as he rises up and forgives us little people on whom he wants to build and does build a community.

Then there was his long-suffering in his Passion. We find him before the high priest's servants and the temple guard after the agony in the Garden, giving them a flash of his Godhead. They came upon him brandishing their swords, and he was very vulnerable; but he asked,

"Whom do you seek?" They replied, "Jesus." He spoke his name, the great name, "I AM." They all fell to the ground, because he spoke his name as God (see Jn 18:6). Then he went back, so to speak, to the human suffering and to the discouragement and the weariness and the deep, deep hurt. Perhaps we do not think of that often enough. In his humanity, Jesus was most vulnerable, most hurtable, because he was perfect.

For us, each small obedience, each little sacrifice that we give to God in whatever he asks of us, each hidden fidelity is a minor resurrection before the divine orchestration of the final Resurrection, his and ours. We rise up, as he did, out of discouragement. We rise up out of our indolence, which he did not have. We rise up out of the shallowness of our understanding. We rise up out of our pride, our self-will, our fear, our trepidation. All of these are resurrections. We know too that each new rising toward a fuller understanding of the mystery of God's love imposes new obligations.

The whole life of Jesus was a rising to the occasion. What we call the great Resurrection is a crown on his lifetime of resurrections. The wonderful thing about our faults, our weaknesses, is that all of them can eventuate in a resurrection. God's grace is there to make this possible.

Tuesday of the Third Week of Lent

❧

I Will Not Violate My Covenant

Psalm 89 speaks of the covenant which God made with his chosen people. Let us consider one of its piercing lines: "I will not violate my covenant, or alter the word that went forth from my lips" (Ps 89:34). Each of us has a baptismal covenant with God. A covenant is a very solemn pact between two persons or two groups. It is a very strong word that perhaps in our times does not carry the force it carried in past centuries. In bygone ages, when a person broke a legal covenant, terrible penalties were imposed.

There were various kinds of materials on which the covenant was written. It could be inscribed on the very best parchment. Sometimes a covenant was cut into stone. There could also be a covenant of trust, an agreement based on a trust so deep that nothing is written down materially. Then we have the covenant of the heart.

In our covenant of baptism we can consider all of these expressions. How would you alter the expression of a covenant on parchment? It could be by adding words that were not originally there. Or it could be by obliterating words in favor of other words. For instance, we might add the word "sometimes". This would be to alter the covenant. We could add "when possible" to the covenant of obedience, of poverty, of chaste love, of spiritual life. We could alter the covenant by a very small word: "if". We could alter the covenant by adding the words "when convenient". We know how Saint Francis cried out, "I, little Brother Francis, promise obedience", and how Saint Clare always echoed his words with love. In this covenant there was never a "sometimes", "when convenient", "if possible", or even an "if". His covenant was total. Her covenant was total. She never added anything to it. She never altered it with additions. She never altered it by obliterating certain words and substituting others.

When a covenant is engraved into stone, one could alter that covenant by chipping it away. On a spiritual level, external infidelity or carelessness chips away at the covenant. Or it can be washed away. We know how water can wear away a stone. Water is so weak and stone so strong; but it is a wondrous thing to behold that a little fountain dripping, dripping, dripping or running very slowly onto a stone will put a groove into it. This could be done on a spiritual level by a persistent little flow of hidden interior infidelities—the dark thoughts. These are frightening considerations, and they are meant to be, so that we realize the horror of altering a covenant, of adjusting, of manipulating the truth.

How could we violate what we call a covenant of trust? We once heard about some very fine contractors who said that when their father put up a building, it was done on a handshake of absolute trust. That could be violated by the person not keeping his word. We can certainly see how this applies to our covenant. This covenant of trust is a covenant of eyes, a covenant of lips and of the spirit. "Yes, I will do it. I will follow your plan. I accept your plans, O beloved divine Architect." We would violate this covenant of trust by not keeping our word, by looking the other way. We can do this in our spiritual life by a nonfocusing on Jesus, with whom the covenant is made at our baptism. We would do that by speaking other names to ourselves oftener than his. Of course the worst possible name that endangers the covenant when spoken oftener than the name of Jesus is "I". This is the violation of the covenant.

Our covenant is a welding of hearts. God says to us, just as he did to David, as he did to his children of the Old Testament, "I will never violate my covenant." He says again and again in different places, "I made a covenant with them. I promised. I will never violate it." God never has. The other party in this heart-welding covenant is myself. The only possibility of violating the covenant lies with me. This terrible power (or to look at it from a brighter perspective, this wonderful power) pertains only to each of us. This is to be what presses us on in our life of love. God says, "I will never violate this covenant." Our whole life must be saying, "Neither will I." My life is not a matter of, "I have to do this, and I have to do that, and vows bind me to this and to that", but, "I have a covenant." This is such a beautiful way to respond to God, who in every call within the call is saying, "I will never violate my covenant."

The covenanted person, who perhaps has been tempted to chip away at the covenant, to obliterate some words in the covenant, or to add some words to the covenant, but comes racing back to make amends, is really keeping the covenant. We should not refuse ourselves the joy of being a covenanted person, growing each day in the keeping of the covenant, coming to see more and more that each little invitation to sacrifice, to love, to fidelity is a keeping of the covenant.

No one who has been occupied with trying to change the words of the covenant, to add this little "sometime", "if", "when convenient", has ever been joyful. Just as we can always find something to complain about if we want to, we can always find something to rejoice about. If we do not refuse ourselves that joy of being a covenanted person, we shall not deny our community the joy of the energizing and inspiring witness of someone who is keeping the covenant, because it shows. We should show God the courtesy of responding to his cry of, "I will never violate my covenant", by saying, "Neither will I."

Wednesday of the Third Week of Lent

In the Footsteps of Jesus

Saint Athanasius says, "Fit your footsteps to his." How do you fit your footsteps to someone else's? I think one element is that you have to trust the person. You don't want to follow the footsteps or "fit" your footsteps to those of someone you do not completely trust. Here we are talking about the footsteps of the God-Man. A child has the instinct to know that there is something very wonderful about setting its little steps in the footprint of a father. We did this as little children. I know I did. I have seen children walking in the snow, trying to fit their little feet into the footprints of their father and walk in those same steps. I think this is a very deep spiritual instinct expressed by them in a child's way, hopefully to be expressed more and more by us in a spousal way. Where do we want to go except where he is going? We know where he is going. He is always going to do the will of his Father. How strange if we would want to go another way.

He is always going forward to save us. How strange if we were not that eager to be saved in the little events of every day. His footsteps were on the way to the Father. They were unflagging. He always kept going. His footsteps were always unswerving. They went straight ahead in the will of the Father. He knew where he was going: "I came from the Father and have come into the world; again I am leaving the world and going to the Father" (Jn 16:28).

For ourselves, we know that our steps are quite often flagging. We lag. We sit down. We get tired. What are we to do when our footsteps are flagging? There is a simple answer. We get up. Sometimes we become discouraged in a prideful way and we think, "Well, what is the use?" What we are really saying is, "I don't want to make the effort to get up." For us to have unflagging steps fitted to his, we have to be always getting up, because of our weakness, our sinfulness. It could be a wonderful thing indeed never to fall, never to flag, but it is a wonderful thing to get up. This can be a true aspiration for the poor sinners we are: that our footsteps become more unflagging according to how often and how quickly we have gotten up.

Then the second consideration: he was unswerving, he went straight on. At this time of the Church year, we are more acutely aware that we often swerve off a path that is too straight for us, too narrow. The very word is almost onomatopoeic: swerve, go off to the side. Either because of illness or because of overindulgence, persons swerve in their walk. We know we swerve sometimes. So what do we do then? We return to the straight path. We realize by God's enlightenment that we have swerved off the path of our resolve, we have swerved off the way of charity and love, we have swerved off the way of fidelity, and with God's grace, we come back.

The third point is related to both of these: how do we become unflagging? It is by penance. That is the only way. We have to make reparation. If we have been flagging by sitting down to rest by the roadside instead of going on, we have to use effort to get up. It can seem very inviting just to sit there or to continue swerving. With God's grace, we have to accept penance and inflict penance on ourselves so that we can return, so that we can fit our footsteps to his.

Saint Paul tells us in his Letter to the Colossians, "Whatever your task, work heartily" (Col 3:23a). Let us work at fitting our footsteps to the footsteps of Christ, those feet so often weary as we are told in the Scriptures: "Jesus, wearied as he was with his journey, sat down beside the well" (Jn 4:6). We have to work with our whole heart, really work. He had, I dare to say it, to work at our redemption. He worked at our redemption all his life and he worked hardest of all in the last days of his life. Let us work with our whole heart to be more unflagging and more unswerving in fitting our footsteps to his.

Thursday of the Third Week of Lent

Freed from the Hunter's Snare

Our blessed Lord has told us very clearly in the Scriptures, "I am the way, and the truth, and the life" (Jn 14:6). These three definitions of himself, which our dear Savior gives us, are one. He is the Way and the Truth and the Life. He is not just a way to the truth; he is Truth on the way. It is by learning truth along the way that we arrive at the Truth which is Christ. He is Life, but again this is not an entity separate from the other two self-definitions he has given us. He is not a life at which we arrive, but he is Life on the way. As we go forward in the truth toward the fullness of life, we are living more fully all the time. His truth is light, and any untruthfulness is darkness. Now, we are children of light. Christ has told us so. We are called this in the Scriptures, but we are reminded that the children of darkness are a little brighter than the children of light. As children of light, we are at home in the light and we are not at home in the darkness. This explains why we are so miserable when we evade the truth about ourselves, because this is not our state. We are not children of darkness. We are redeemed, we are loved, we are called to eternal life with God. It is astonishing to what length we will go sometimes to divest ourselves of that nobility of being children of light, and with what care we will cultivate the darkness. We will work like little beavers sometimes to cultivate untruth. This is most unrewarding. So let us never dissipate our energies that way.

We want to face ourselves in truth. At least in our saner moments we realize that we don't present too great a picture. We see some things within ourselves that are very difficult to look at. And so our first very human reaction is to look the other way or maybe find somebody whom we think is even less good-looking than ourselves, in order to establish ourselves in a kind of false security. But the only way that we can look at ourselves is in the light of Christ and in the light of a God who loves us. We should put the primary accent on Christ-knowledge rather than on self-knowledge. If we are occupied every day in growing in Christ-knowledge, then self-knowledge will take care of itself. It will appear, and the wonderful thing is that we shall be able to bear it. Let us seek for that Christ-knowledge in the Scriptures, in the events of the day, and with Christ's strength and power let us establish in ourselves the great freedom and lightsomeness of heart that is the truth.

Truth guards us like a shield (see Ps 91:4). This is a very profound statement. We are inclined to think, half-consciously, that truth is something we had better shield ourselves against. This false notion is what gives rise to the syndrome of self-pity, of self-excuse, of condescension, and of all the dreadful things that come in their train: accusations of others, censure of others, and so on. We hold up this false and flimsy shield against the real shield, which is truth. The Lenten liturgy says again and again: He has delivered me from the snare of the hunter and from the arrows that fly at me (see Ps 91:3, 5). It is the truth that does this. Truth is the shield. Lent is the time for facing squarely in the light of Christ-knowledge who my hunters are, who are after me. Each one has her own hunters. There are some hunters common to us all in some degree. But each person has her unique, expert hunters who are laying snares for her holiness. We take up that shield of Christ's truth and are delivered from the sharp arrows of these hunters only if we know who they are. If we think these are our greatest friends instead of those who are hunting down our holiness, then we can never be delivered. But if we can make this beginning of truth in Christ-knowledge, and acknowledge who are our hunters, we can go on quickly from there. And it is a very exhilarating run.

Aggressiveness may be my special hunter. If I am not willing to recognize this as the enemy who is hunting down my holiness, obviously I will never be delivered from the snares of that hunter. The first step is to blush for shame that I am aggressive, and recognize this as a hunter. Or I may be hypersensitive. The least word may send me into some kind of emotional contortion. The first thing I want to do is to say, "This is my hunter. This is the one hunting down my holiness", and take up the shield of truth which is that admission, the shield of Christ who says, "I am the Truth." I need to be shielded against this onslaught and delivered from its snares.

Scripture says, "I can do all things in him who strengthens me" (Phil 4:13). This is not a ticket to presumption. I can do all things in him who strengthens me, all things that are asked of me. I cannot decide that I can do something for which I am completely unequipped. I can't be a trapeze artist because "I can do all things in him who strengthens me." I would have to study; I would have to work quite a while to learn how to be a trapeze artist. Sometimes we see the truth best in these rather ridiculous extreme examples. Once we have been rescued with Christ's love and grace from distortion, then we begin to understand that to say, "I cannot bear what is asked of me", is a final blasphemy. That is quite a statement, isn't it? It is not a culpable blasphemy for the simple reason that we do not have sense enough to know what we are saying when we say things like that. Lent is a marvelous time for growing in sense.

Our Lord said to Saint Paul the equivalent of, "Stop asking questions; my grace is sufficient for you." He didn't say, "Now, bear up, Paul; in six months it is going to be much better." He didn't explain to him why things had to be as they were. He just said, "My grace is sufficient for you" (2 Cor 12:9). This is always what God says to us. Whatever he asks of us, whatever inspirations he gives us the impulse to follow, his grace is sufficient. In any infirmities he sends, his grace is sufficient for us. It would be a blasphemy to say God sends us a suffering that we are not able to bear. This is never true.

Why should I bear the burden of myself? Because this is the burden that God chose in his infinite wisdom, his omniscience, and his omnipotence, though he was perfectly free to make me any way he wanted, to arrange any kind of situation in life for me that he wished. Therefore it is a wonderful thing if I face it in truth. It is only when I wrestle and go through all manner of gymnastics to throw off this burden that I am really miserable. When I face the fact of myself in the light of Christ's love, then I am free. I want to sing and dance and be grateful because God can love a person like me, because others are willing to go on living with a person like me.

Friday of the Third Week of Lent

I Will Not Take Back My Love

A FEW DAYS AGO we considered Psalm 89 in which God says, "I will not take my love from him, nor will I ever betray my faithfulness. I will not violate my covenant or alter what my lips have uttered" (Ps 89:34, NIV). Let us linger on the first of these promises, to which we desire to respond, "I will not take back *my* love."

How do we take back our love? I would like to ponder three ordinary ways that we take back our love. We take back our love often enough, and we do not know it, in the little seeming obstacles from without. We are determined to love God fully and perfectly, with all of our being, with all of our strength, as God asks of us in the commandments, but then a circumstance or situation comes along, and we take back our love. We weren't expecting this. I trust it is very humiliating (and would pray it is humbling as well) to realize what little obstacles can entice us to take back our love. Then there are things within us that entice us to take back our love. The third point is the deeply moving paradox that if love is not always growing, we will be taking it back. Love is never static. If it is not growing each day, then it is being taken back. It is shriveling; it is withering in that measure.

In Psalm 69 (Grail translation) the psalmist makes a great cry, "Ransom me, oppressed by my foes." Who are my foes? I think our worst foes are those forces within us that try to make us believe that our best friends are foes. God, as it were, extends his friendliness, his desire that we go forward in love, by giving us this little unexpected situation, this little unanticipated trial. These are friendly things in God's program of each day: this is how you can love more; this is how you can grow in love. These are friends, but often enough, we consider them our foes. We think we must clear the path of all these "foes" that obstruct our program for holiness. In reality these are our friends.

God explains in Psalm 89 through the mouth of the psalmist how we do not respond to him who never takes back his love. He says, "They refuse to walk as I decree." The situations of every day are what he decrees, and we stomp our feet like obstinate children: "No, I don't want to go that way." But that is the way he decrees. "They refuse to walk as I decree." It is frightening to read it, yet how easily we do it. Then he outlines for us what he will do to those who refuse to keep his commands. He says he will "punish them with a rod", and he will "scourge them on account of their guilt". Then God, being God, immediately adds, "I will not take my love from him, nor will I ever betray my faithfulness." We want to look for the places where we betray our faithfulness. "O God, I will love you forever and ever, but not in this." And so I take back my love on this occasion, in this seeming obstacle, in this friendly little event that I mistake for a foe.

What are the foes within that want to entice us to take back our love? Perhaps our moodiness, our mood swings. Today I love God with all my heart, and then tomorrow I am feeling depressed, discouraged; I am tempted, which is the common lot of all men. Our dear Lord was discouraged in the Garden of Gethsemane. He had to do something about it. No one was ever so tempted to discouragement as he who sweat blood over it. He had that great temptation of saying: "What's the use? All this suffering for men, some of whom will not respond." He was often tempted to sadness, but we never see him depressed. He always went forward in his love, never taking it back.

Finally, we can take back our love by failing to make it grow every day. The seemingly untoward circumstances from without, or the sometimes miasmic fumes within us, are dealt with by doing more. Every time that I do not take back my love when there is something to oppose my own plan, my own desire, my own idea of holiness, then love, ipso facto, increases. Every little sacrifice accepted and offered, every situation that seems untoward but is met as a friend, will help us grow in faith, in holiness, and in love. Each time, with God's grace, I put down the inimical forces within myself, I am stronger. Conversely, every time I stop before an obstacle, my love grows weaker. Every time I indulge those debilitating forces within me, my love grows weaker. A muscle that is not growing stronger every day from being used is growing weaker. A mind that is not exercised every day is not remaining on its own level of intelligence but growing weaker. Every force within us either grows in vigor and expands, or it grows more languid and diminishes. This is true above all of love. This is the only way that we don't take back our love: by allowing it to grow every day.

Saturday of the Third Week of Lent

Love's Resolve

What was the attitude of Christ as he entered upon his Passion? This is the Jesus who had said, "Learn from me; for I am gentle and lowly in heart" (Mt 11:29). This is such a difficult lesson for our proud little minds and our hearts, so very facile and quick with excuses and ready pardon for ourselves. He told us what his attitude was toward all that was about to happen: "He who sent me is with me; he has not left me alone, for I always do what is pleasing to him" (Jn 8:29). It was just as simple as that. The simple things seem staggering to us, because we are full of excuses. The attitude of Jesus was to do always the things that please the Father, who has never stopped loving us, who has never stopped hoping in us, who has thought us worth saving and so has never stopped hoping and trying. This was Jesus' attitude right up to that last cry on the Cross, "It is finished." He was still hoping and trying and believing. What men might call the failures of his earthly life were these marvelous triumphs at his death: it was a forgiven woman of the streets who stood by him; it was a criminal who talked about his being King, for only kings have kingdoms. For him these were great triumphs, as it is for him when he manages at last to get his love and his forgiveness through the mists and the layers of our stupidity, our wrong responses, our pettiness, our lack of gratitude.

As Lent speeds by, let us go forward with some positive action, and take the right position. Who had the right position? The publican (see Lk 18:9–14). He was in the back pew (or whatever accommodations they had in the temple), and his head was bent. Certainly he looked up at that Pharisee. He could have undoubtedly made some remarks about the Pharisee. He could have said to God, "I do not boast like he is doing." But real truth is always received with a bent head, which is the expression of a bent heart. A head held high in pride will never be able to allow God to forgive it. Real truth is received with a bent head and on bended knees. Scripture tells us we can be made white as wool, white as snow (see Is 1:18), but we have to take the stand of the publican and say, "Yes, my faults are scarlet; yes, my faults are really crimson red." If we go on pretending that they are only pink or that somebody spilled something on us, then we cannot be forgiven because we do not allow God to forgive us.

Jesus is saying wordlessly all during the Passion, and verbally after his Resurrection: "Was it not necessary that the Christ should suffer these things and enter into his glory?" (Lk 24:26). If the Redeemer could say this, then what should we say who are not the Redeemer but the ones needing redemption? Ought we not to suffer for our faults and our sins? Ought it not to be the clean suffering of saying, "Yes, these are my sins. It is not anybody else's fault. Ought I not to suffer?" This is a very salvific suffering.

Scripture says, "He was spurned and avoided by men, a man of suffering, accustomed to infirmity, one of those from whom men hide their faces, spurned, and we held him in no esteem" (Is 53:3, NAB). He knew all about it. He was the one held in no esteem. How much we want to be held in esteem sometimes. But what is it to be held in God's esteem? It is to be with the publican asking for forgiveness with a bent head, beating one's breast. This is what it is to be held in God's esteem, as he shows us clearly in the Scriptures.

Jeremiah says, "When I found your words I devoured them; they became my joy and the happiness of my heart" (Jer 15:16, NAB). His words may not presently suit my intellectual digestion, but they do fully suit my spiritual digestion if I will allow them. Jeremiah says, and I think this is the key word, "When I *found* your words". Jeremiah doesn't say, "When I read your words, when I heard your words". This is important, yes, but we can read the Passion and we can hear the Passion, and never quite find the Passion. How much we can read, how much we can hear without really finding. May this coming week be a week of high resolve. High resolve means our resolve will not flag. If it staggers, it will straighten up. If it tends to fall, it will hold on to grace and get up again. The prophet said, "I have set my face like flint" (Is 50:7). Let us set our hearts like love's flint.

FOURTH WEEK OF LENT

Fourth Sunday of Lent, Year A

A Parable in Reverse

Our dear Lord often spoke to the crowds in parables. When his disciples had him to themselves later on, they would ask what the parable meant, and he would explain the deep truth that it expressed. This is reversed in the Gospel of Laetare Sunday when we read the long passage from Saint John about the man born blind who was cured by Jesus (see Jn 9:1–41). It is a heavenly story; it is a very earthy story. We see these ambitious, self-centered Pharisees, and we see the man who was cured showing remarkable inner strength. Then we see his nervous parents gladly referring the explanation to him. This is a human situation that our dear Lord is asking us to understand also as a parable.

The man was blind and he was cured; we are sinful and we are forgiven. But we are only able to confess our sins and our faults because we know we will be forgiven. I think this is something we should ponder very deeply. On our own, we would not want to confess our sins unless we were already assured of forgiveness. When our dying Lord said, "Father, forgive them. They do not know what they are doing", he was not only speaking of his immediate executioners, but he was speaking of us. Even before that, when we were conceived in the mind of God, and surely this is a great mystery, he knew what we would do, how we would react, the times we would fall, the sins we would commit. In considering the profound spiritual truth that we are enabled to confess our sins because we know we will be forgiven by God, we see also that in community living we are able to be honest about our failings because we know that the persons to whom we confess these things have already forgiven us.

In today's Gospel we are pondering the parable drawn from an actual human event, rather than a truth drawn from a parable, as in other parts of the Gospel. The man who was blind was questioned, "Are you the beggar?" He said, "I am." In the parable, when we have that reassurance that God forgives us, then we can say, "I am the one who did it." The Gospel story is so familiar to us that perhaps we don't quite realize the courage of this man. He was very forthright after he had been given his sight. The Pharisees were persons to be dealt with. It is amazing the way he spoke to them. He was literally taking his life in his hands. You can almost hear their teeth gnashing as he asked them in common modern parlance, "Don't you get it? What is the matter? Look, I was blind; now I see. This is a really great person." They interrogated him further. He gave that delightful answer. You can imagine his shoulders shrugging as he said, "All I know is that before I could not see, and now I see." It is as simple as that. From this, too, we draw a spiritual parable for ourselves: we do not analyze, we do not blame our miseries on others, but when we know that we have been wrong and we are able to confess it because we know we are forgiven, then we, too, in a wonderful and greatly dignified spiritual way can shrug our shoulders and say, "All I know is that whereas before I was blind, now I see." I think this is at the heart of real conversion.

Then we move on in the spiritual parable that we draw from the real human story. The man born blind questioned Jesus, "Who is he, Lord, that I may believe in him?" Our Lord answered with supreme majesty, "You have seen him and the one speaking with you is he." When our Lord pronounced this most majestic word, almost saying his name, I AM, the man worshipped him. Life has become so simple, so very simple. It is never God who makes our lives complicated or morose or unhappy. It is we who do it by not realizing the grace of being forgiven, being freed to confess the truth about ourselves because we have been forgiven.

A person who has been forgiven is a happy person, a person who is at ease. There is a great freedom that comes of knowing that I am loved not because people have this great picture of me that I know in my inmost heart is not accurate. It is the happiness of knowing that they see me at my worst and they still love me. This is what we have first of all with God; and then being so close in community or family life, we have this with one another. We know each other quite well. We don't know the inmost struggles of the heart or the secret victories or the painful falls, but we know a great deal. Each of us has the assurance: "I am loved, even though those around me know what I am really like." This is a great freedom. Spiritually we still grieve for our sins and our faults, but we go forward when we are forgiven.

There is a legend, which is certainly deeply rooted in truth, that Saint Peter, having wept at cockcrow at the denials that were instigated by his weakness, wept so much throughout his life that he wept furrows into his cheeks. This is a beautiful legend, a beautiful spiritual truth, perhaps even a physical truth. But Peter didn't just sit there and weep. He went out and he preached and he taught. He was a pilgrim going from place to place, and he suffered and he died. When we have real contrition, it is never inert. It is never something that in any way invites us to melancholy, much less to despair, but it begets in us a new intention to do and to suffer for Christ. We see that especially in Peter.

In the Gospel for Laetare Sunday our Lord is giving us an actual happening and letting us take for ourselves the spiritual parable of our own blindness or sinfulness, which he heals. In being healed of blindness we find new courage. I think we can be confident that this blind beggar would in no way have spoken to those Pharisees like that if he hadn't been cured by the Lord. A great courage comes with being forgiven. Perhaps the parents were so frightened because they hadn't been forgiven enough or hadn't been forgiven yet.

There is such tremendous depth here. Unlike the apostles, we don't have to say, "Explain this parable to us." It is as though our dear Lord is saying to us, "Now tell me how you understand the parable." When we confess our sinfulness, we know that we have been forgiven. If we understand what sinfulness is and what forgiveness is, then we hurry forward. We weep in our hearts, but we do not sit down and weep. We are on the move. It will be wonderful in eternity to know just what this blind man did afterward.

Fourth Sunday of Lent, Year B

Filling Up the Sufferings of Christ

The Scriptures tell us again and again that our redemption is accomplished—it is finished, it is done. "He delivered us from the dominion of darkness and transferred us to the kingdom of his beloved Son" (Col 1:13). We are a redeemed people. Yet Scripture also says that "in my flesh I am filling up what is lacking in the afflictions of Christ on behalf of his body, which is the Church" (Col 1:24, NAB). All through Lent we are being invited very urgently by the liturgy to make wholehearted choices, to struggle, to put on the armor of holiness, to go out armed for the battle. The ancient name for Lent is "the season of the battle", *agonia*, which was the Greek word for the final testing of the athlete or the warrior, and has become the term for the Agony in the Garden. I think we can reconcile these two facets by very human analogies. They are not perfect, but I do think they are understandable.

God has made it possible that we should be redeemed. He has removed the obstacles. He has taken away the penalties, which none of us could pay. Our Lord has made satisfaction to the Father, which not one of us or all of us together could make, which not even his most blessed and Immaculate Mother could make. He has made it possible that we should live in the light, be drawn out of the power of darkness. The fact that he has delivered us from the power of darkness is not to say that we cannot give ourselves back to the power of darkness. The fact that we are redeemed in no way circumscribes our human free will, our choice.

A very common human analogy would be the father of an artist who provides every advantage when he recognizes a great talent in his child. He gives him the best courses, he gives him the time to study, he gives him the materials with which to work, he makes possible all manner of inspirations for him; and all that remains to be done is that, as the child grows in this learning and inspiration, he executes what was made possible for him. There still remains a choice. He could be slothful and say, "I don't feel like painting." He could be sensual and say, "It's too much work." He could be proud and say, "Perhaps I will never equal da Vinci or Michelangelo, and therefore I will not paint." There could be any number of reasons. But this is not to say that the father has not provided for the genius of this child, that he has not done everything possible for him to execute his genius, that he has not provided him with inspiration and with opportunity. In a similar way, as I said, God has made it possible that we should be redeemed, but this in no way circumscribes our human free will, our choice.

Another analogy is found in music, where there is a note called the tonic and a note called the dominant in every musical key. The tonic note in any key is where the melody comes to rest. It is like the foundation note. Then there is the dominant note, which recurs again and again, and the notes in the tonic chord always reach to the dominant. I think that's a good way to envision Lent: the tonic is penance and the dominant is love, and love comes to rest on the penance, which is the foundation of Lent. The tonic note is always reaching to the dominant which is the redeeming love of Christ. If we just sat on the tonic note we would never have a melody. In the same way, we have this profound theology of Lent: it is "all done", and yet it is now *being done* by us.

What does it mean to fill up the afflictions of Christ? He left nothing undone. But the Apostle adds, "for his Body, which is the Church". This is a truth that should spur us on, one on which we can never meditate enough. There is for each of us in the Passion of Christ something to be filled up for his Body which is the Church. His redemption of the human race was a perfect act to which as human beings we can add nothing. It was a divine act, but it was also a human act by the Head of the Mystical Body. In the human act of redemption, there is a measure for each of us to contribute. Surely we are more conscious than ever before of the needs of the suffering Body of the Church, and that each of us has a measure to fill. This is in our power and we cannot deny it.

Fourth Sunday of Lent, Year C

High Quality Waiting

In today's liturgy Saint Paul tells us about the new creation and the old things passing away (see 2 Cor 5:17). We have old and dreary faults. We have an old pattern of going wrong ways in the little challenges of every day, and this pattern has to pass away. Let us wince, where this is appropriate, at the old things that we do not want to retain. God's new creation is clear to us. He wants us to be holy. He wants us to give ourselves entirely to him in the little and large challenges of every day, to seize upon all the opportunities for repentance.

In the Gospel we have that most beloved presentation of the Prodigal Son (see Lk 15:1–32). Yes, he was prodigal in wrongdoing, he was prodigal in wasting; but there was a prodigal father who was so prodigal in love, so prodigal in mercy. The father watched at the window. That is beautiful, but it is a little bit unusual, because usually it is the woman who is watching at the window. It is the woman, the spouse, the mother especially, who is always waiting for the beloved child to come back home to God. This is a woman's particular office: to watch at the window, to be a hard-hoper, never to give up. Probably everyone in the household of the prodigal son had given up. They never thought they would see him again, and perhaps most of them were just as happy about that. But the father went on waiting.

A bride also waits, as we read in the Song of Songs, "The voice of my beloved! Behold, he comes, leaping upon the mountains, bounding over the hills" (Song 2:8). But again, we reverse that, because it is really the Beloved who waits for us. What does he wait for? He waits for us to come stumbling down the path of truth from which we have veered by every deliberate fault. He waits for our repentance. He waits to forgive us. Is that not wonderful to consider?

If, in the light of Lenten graces, we discover little resentments in our hearts about this situation or this person or this reaction, we want to look into the quality of our waiting. If there is any measure for our love, this is it. How long are we willing to wait for the unfolding of God's plans in the situations we do not understand? How long are we willing to wait for others to come to the fullness of God's plan for them? How long are we willing to wait in an active waiting for our poor selves? It is not virtue to get into a perfect fury of rage at ourselves that we are not perfect. This would be our ticket to more imperfect behavior.

Let us then in this week be occupied with improving the quality of our waiting, and in being more grateful than ever for God's waiting for us. Oh, what would become of us if God did not wait for us? May we be more that new creation in this new week of Lent. May the stale old things, the stale old faults and the stale old misspendings of grace pass away. We can come into the new creation, happily stumbling down the road to say, "I have no right to be in the house of God. Could I just be a servant here?" God will open his divine arms and throw a party of grace for our homecoming. In high quality waiting, we wait upon the Lord—wait upon his hour, wait for one another, wait for the answer to prayer.

Rejoicing in the Lord

In the reading at Lauds yesterday from the prophet Nehemiah, we were told the most marvelous thing about Sunday and every day. It is remarkable that the prophet says, "Rejoicing in the Lord must be your strength" (Neh 8:10, NAB). In the Church's greatest penitential season she is not saying that our strength will be in herculean penance. Certainly she is saying penance is very important, but she is not saying our greatest strength will be there. She is not saying in these forty days of fast that our strength will be in rigorous fasting. Certainly strength comes from abstention, from self-control, but she is not saying that is where our greatest strength will be. She is not even saying that our strength will be in prolonged prayer. Certainly the Church is saying constantly, "Pray, pray, pray", and our strength will be there. But all of these things, if they are true and sincere, are part of rejoicing. If we are doing penance rightly, we do it joyfully. The fasting is a joyful thing. If prayer is real, it will never make us somber. It will make us joyful.

Holy Mother Church brings these threads together, these beautiful threads of her tapestry of union with God, and says, "Rejoicing in the LORD must be your strength." The more we center our joy in Jesus, the stronger we are, the firmer we are in the little storms of life that must come to us all, the little and large sufferings, disappointments, frustrations. But we are not deterred by these things, because it is not in our plans and their fulfillment that our joy lies—some little or large satisfactions, yes, but not our joy. Our joy must be in him, where alone things have permanent depth and even eternality. The more earnestly we live our Lent, the more will we be finding our joy in Jesus. Then we will be strong, for the prophet has said, "Rejoicing in the LORD must be your strength." So let us rejoice. "Laetare", the Church sang out yesterday. She will tell us to bow our heads again, but only so that we can raise them in glory and wonder at Easter, because in him is all our joy. If we focus all our joy in Jesus, we will never be confounded. That is why we will be so strong. So rejoice in the Lord that you may be strong, and be strong because you rejoice in the Lord.

We think of the eternal rejoicing among the three Persons of the Blessed Trinity, which from time immemorial has been symbolized by a circle. A circle is a beautiful thing, yet we also have the expression "a vicious circle". We know what is meant by that. It relates to the way we usually use the phrase, "one thing leads to another". We almost always use that phrase in a negative way, which is often true: this little infidelity, another infidelity, a larger infidelity, a gross infidelity, perhaps an ultimate infidelity. One thing leads to another. But there is another way of thinking of that, the affirmative way. One thing does lead to another. One good example does lead to another. One act of kindness does lead to another. It does set up a circle of virtue and restores to its rightful place the symbol of the Blessed Trinity that is the circle. A circle is something that is completely united, that has no beginning or end, and in which all the points are equally and beautifully distant from the center. Do you remember that incident from the life of the great Giotto? He was asked to draw something for the Pope as a special gift for him. He drew a circle on paper. The interlocutor was horrified. "This is the gift you have for the Pope?" Giotto said, "But it's a perfect circle." For an artist to draw a perfect circle freehand is a great thing. It was a gift worthy of a Pope: a perfect circle, symbol of the Blessed Trinity.

TUESDAY OF THE FOURTH WEEK OF LENT

Caught Foxes

WE HEAR AGAIN AND AGAIN in Lent a very forthright word: "Cease to do evil" (Is 1:16). How do we think of evil? Most of us think of the violence in the world, the terrible defiance in the Church—not just the lack of loyalty and fidelity to our Holy Father, but people heaping insults upon the Vicar of Christ. We think of nations devouring each other with their own greed, their own desires. These are indeed great evils, and we must mourn for them. We must bring sacrificial offerings to assuage them. Every act of peaceful love is doing something to alleviate the terrors of war. Each new giving of life to others by our understanding, our sympathy, our example, is doing something for torn families, for torn nations.

Compared to the evils of the world scene, our own failings may seem insignificant, but we do not want to be deflected from seeing how destructive they are. While pondering the words, "Cease to do evil", I thought of the words from the Song of Songs, "Catch the little foxes that make havoc of the vineyard" (see Song 2:15). There are predatory animals that seek to destroy the vineyard of the Church but will never succeed, animals that leap, as it were, upon the person of Christ's Vicar to wound and assault him. There are the great, destructive, ferocious animals of evil that leap at the throat of the world and strangle its peace. There are the little foxes in our own lives, and these make havoc of the vineyard.

What are the little foxes in my own spiritual life that make havoc of my vineyard and, through the vineyard of my own heart, make havoc of the community? One of the dangers of little foxes is that we are not very afraid of them. We draw back or we run from a large, ferocious, predatory bird or animal, but we can fail to fear these little foxes. They are so small, and that is their very power. They can get into the smallest crevice of our heart, of our soul. As we go in search of them, I would like to suggest three, so that we may recognize the little foxes in order to catch them, to stop them from making havoc in the vineyard.

First of all, we can consider that little fox which is a pouting heart. A heart is made to pour itself out. This little fox of a pouting heart turns right in on itself to stay in the dank atmosphere that it creates. It begets a closedness to love, truly a frightening expression. Of its nature, love is a pouring forth. So a pouting heart is a little fox that indeed makes havoc of the vineyard of our lives.

Then there is that little fox of an irresolute spirit. We are full of good spiritual plans and resolutions, but the very resolutions are irresolute. As soon as something comes to confront that resolution we can waver, and we don't carry through. This is a little fox. This little fox tries to break the connection between my resolution, inspired by the Holy Spirit in prayer, and the present situation. The little foxes are perhaps most clever about breaking connections: I want to suffer great things for God, but that has nothing to do with the present moment, with the sacrifice I am called to make, with this overcoming of myself, this reaching out in understanding. An animal as small as a mouse can eat away a wire connection and the whole circuit is ruined, and all the lights are out and all the heat is gone. We need very much to guard against that little fox of an irresolute spirit. Love is never static. We want to make the connection about how love can be made stronger by this very overcoming of myself in these little day-by-day situations.

A pouting heart, an irresolute spirit—and very related to these is a closed mind: I allow a little fox to slam shut the door of my mind, so that I don't see what this little secret overcoming of myself has to do with the growth of my community or family, with all that we are supposed to be to the world, in taking to ourselves the hardships and miseries of all men and women. The mind can be closed against this tiny little hardship of a relationship, of a circumstance, of a situation in the day. The little fox rejoices to have flung the door shut.

I ask that we look deeply this Lenten day into ourselves and see what little foxes are making havoc and need to be caught and destroyed. We all have these little foxes to catch. A picture comes into my mind, flashed on the screen of memory from years ago. We had a whole box of books in the parlor. I opened it and found all these little tiny pieces of paper. Every book was chewed through: just one little mouse had been making havoc of that whole box. I saw the horror of what this one little mouse had done. If one tiny creature can make havoc of a whole box, then what can the nonphysical evil do? So cease doing evil and catch the foxes: the pouting heart, the irresolute spirit, the closed mind.

Wednesday of the Fourth Week of Lent

Beauty and Penance

When we examine the Church's liturgy, the idea of blossoming beauty is very evident everywhere in this season of penance. It neither begins nor ends with anything severe, even though we are told to set ourselves to work, which will inevitably involve suffering and pain since we are so disjointed. We are so unbeautiful sometimes. The Lenten liturgy is one of hope and of restoration that speaks of a great blossoming that is to come, that is to be accomplished during these days. Holy Church tells us that it is not in vain that we keep vigil, and that a crown is promised to those who watch. She tells us that our penance is not without purpose.

We might stop to reflect there for just a minute. In our time the Church has lifted so much of what was mandatory in penitential practices, thereby placing great trust in us. She has not changed anything about her concept of penance or understanding of the need for penance, she has merely removed penalties. She has tried to show us a greater trust. If the Church is aware that penance had been done for the wrong reason, she is now asking us to do it for the right reason, without penalty. Sometimes there is confusion about this.

The Church says precisely in her hymn at Lauds that "This day comes, your day, in which everything blossoms again." There is already a very deep theology of creation in that line: everything shall flower again. Nothing different is to be made; but something already in us will flower again, something created beautiful and sometimes spoiled or distorted, will be restored. Creation will reassume its original beauty, its original meaning.

If we were to define beauty, we would come, sooner or later, to a sense of congruousness: what is proper to a thing, what is congruous to parts working with parts. What do we mean when we say that a person is physically beautiful? We mean there is a congruity: everything is where it belongs, everything is in excellent form. When we have elements out of place, then we have something unbeautiful, distorted, something that repels us, at least at first sight. Beauty and grace of motion derive from congruity of the parts. They work smoothly with one another, part with part.

It is the same in the moral realm, in the spiritual realm. Moral beauty is truth, the congruity of truth. It is congruous to itself, congruous in all its parts. In physical nature or among persons, the basis of everything comic is incongruity. It is something that does not make sense. Sometimes it is said that humor is based on a sense of the incongruous. This is true of humor in the spiritual sense. But in the moral realm we want a congruity of truth. In the spiritual realm we want a congruousness of holiness.

There are several kinds of physical beauty. When we have touched the spirit of a person, what is physical is changed in our eyes. There are few things that more quickly lose their appeal than mere outer beauty. It doesn't stand up very long. In the end it can become very specious because when the moral congruousness is not there, when the spirit is not beautiful, there is almost a certain resentment that a person should look beautiful when we have discovered such a lack of interior beauty. On the other hand, we have all had the experience that when we come to love and to understand someone, when we come to touch the spirit of another person, we can't bear that this person should be thought unbeautiful by anyone else, because we recognize the beauty there so easily.

This doesn't work both ways: outer beauty does not beget inner beauty. Inner beauty does project outward beauty. Inner beauty transfigures even the outward appearance. But it does not work the other way. In fact, it works in just the opposite way: a beautiful shell over a lack of inner beauty is almost repulsive because it is so incongruous with the spirit. We want to work toward congruousness of spirit and of moral truth within, the acceptance of truth, the acceptance of doing the right thing for the right reason in our spiritual life, so that we establish an inner beauty.

When we say a person has an awkward walk we mean that there is not congruity of movement, the limbs do not work together in coordination. We often walk awkwardly in our spiritual lives because we are not living congruously; and so we become "comic", in a very dark sense of the word, because we are not congruous. All our failures in virtue can be reduced to this lack of beauty, this inconsistency within ourselves. Because of human weakness and limitations, we will always be inconsistent on occasion, and particularly in our own weakest areas, but we cannot afford to live inconsistently with ourselves. Least of all can we afford to deny the inconsistency, because this is already to be unbeautiful.

To return to the liturgy, not only does the Church begin her Lenten liturgies with enthusiasm for a great reflowering of beauty, but she establishes almost immediately her theology of penance. The Lauds hymn, "O Sol Salutis, Intime", speaks in a very poetic figure of the tears of repentance welling up from the heart if the rod of penance breaks its stubborn rock. To me that hymn is a whole theology of penance, most beautifully expressed. There is a reason for everything we do, and every dying in Lent is a dying toward resurrection. All the penances or restrictions establish a truth, and beauty and truth cannot be separated. Every lack of beauty is some kind of untruth, and every kind of untruth, spiritual or moral, is a sin against beauty. It is important to think about and remember that. The more truthful we are in our spiritual life, the more beautiful it becomes. We become beautiful only by an increase of acceptance of the responsibility to live in the truth. This is what our Lenten program is meant to be.

Thursday of the Fourth Week of Lent

The Paradox of Penance

In order to make an attempt toward a reflowering of beauty in our own lives in this springtime season, it is necessary to take the responsibility for our own goodness and for our own beauty. It is a paradox, and yet a profound truth, that if we agree to dislike ourselves, we relieve ourselves of the responsibility for ourselves. That sounds like a complicated sentence, so let's go through it again. If we do not like ourselves, if we agree to dislike ourselves, then we are relieved of the effort to improve ourselves. Let me give you an example.

Years ago I read about a missionary order, cofounded by two priests. One of these was a very delightful person in many ways, but he was fond of telling the young seminarians to remember that they were "cesspools of iniquity". He would catch one of the fellows and ask him if he knew that he was a cesspool of iniquity. Most of them replied, "Yes, Father, I am a cesspool of iniquity." But one day a seminarian said, "No, Father, I am a temple of God." The founder was a good man, but obviously tainted with the Jansenism of the time. If we agree to this image of ourselves as a cesspool of iniquity, what could we ever expect of ourselves? We would disclaim all responsibility for growth and especially for beauty.

To continue with this very unlovely figure that he used, we would expect a cesspool to be full of stench, and so we wouldn't be ashamed to commit fault upon fault, to act unbeautifully. Self-depreciation begets all kinds of faults and sins, including serious carnal sins: gluttony, slovenliness, slothfulness, and in the end, unchastity. When we don't like ourselves, we are also very easily a prey to envy, to jealousy, to vindictiveness, to sullenness, to resentfulness of other people. This is only what you would expect of this kind of area. But if you accept the image of yourself as a temple of God, then by that acceptance you immediately take on a tremendous responsibility. A temple of God has to be kept shining and clean and uncluttered and beautiful. The money changers that keep coming back have to be driven out all the time. This place that is to be called a house of prayer has to be made prayerful all the time. And so in agreeing to love ourselves, to appreciate ourselves, we show ourselves humble enough to take on the responsibility for our own lives and for our own growth before God. So never think that it is very humble to say that you are perfectly contemptible. If we are perfectly contemptible, then we can be expected to act in a contemptible way. But if we accept ourselves as a beautiful creation of God, called to see him and to love him and to be with him forever, then we have a great responsibility.

When our behavior is sometimes contemptible, we will suffer from this very much, and we will determine to do something about it.

The first step in trying to grow beautiful is to accept ourselves as created beautiful, called to be beautiful and called to be great. If we don't like ourselves, then inevitably this will spawn dislike of other people. But when we have accepted responsibility for ourselves, when we have the security of knowing that we are created beautiful, whatever our failures are, whatever the ways we have defaced ourselves, then we have the power to become increasingly beautiful. We are meant to be beautiful, and we have the power, as Saint Paul says, "to rekindle the gift of God" (2 Tim 1:6). We have the power, with God's grace, to realize his ambition. We have the power to come up to God's expectations. I don't see how we could envy anyone when we see the greatness and the potential for greatness within ourselves, a greatness that no one else can ever attain for the simple reason that no one else can be I.

When we agree to accept this and to understand that this, and not self-contempt, is the beginning of humility, then the love of other people follows. I don't mean that we do not commit faults—obviously we do, but there is a difference of orientation, there is a completely different philosophy and theology. So we begin with this acceptance of ourselves and of our great responsibility. This then begets congruousness in our lives.

Let us look deeply into the liturgy, and let us pray for one another, that at the end of this Lent we may be more beautiful to one another, more responsible for the goodness that is in us, more appreciative of what it is possible for us to be in God's sight.

Friday of the Fourth Week of Lent

Almsgiving

Saint Leo the Great says that almsgiving is a "profitable companion of spiritual fasting". I was stopped by that adjective "profitable". The saint is obviously speaking of almsgiving as being profitable to ourselves, as well as to the one to whom the alms are given. This is deeply and profoundly true: almsgiving is profitable for ourselves. It is a paradoxical profit, because the more we give of ourselves, the more we have. This bank account grows by decreasing. Every time we draw out of ourselves what is in us to give, the interior bank account is enlarged. It is a wondrous spiritual phenomenon. On the other hand, the more we keep of ourselves for ourselves, the more impoverished we are, the more unprofitable is our manner of living.

I would like to consider some practical ways in which we give alms, beginning with the local church of the family. First of all, there is the almsgiving of space. Now, what do I mean by space? We are very, very parsimonious sometimes in how much space we will give one another to grow—to grow in understanding, to grow spiritually. We can parcel and box one another in, as it were, withholding from others the space of our love that allows them to grow. Everyone needs space to grow, the space of our understanding, but we can be very niggardly, not giving space to others because we are keeping it all for ourselves. "I need lots of space. I can't be confined. I can't be over-disciplined. I cannot be kept this way. I have to have spaciousness!" The more I keep for myself, the more demanding I am of others. As a homilist once jocosely said, "I'm all in favor of change—other people should definitely change." We are always ready to say *what* they should change, too. But if our love creates spaciousness around each one, then she can grow in a way that she will not be able to grow if we deprive her of the space of our love and understanding.

There is also the almsgiving of time. I mean this not only in the sense of giving our time, because none of us has a prodigious amount of this! We can, though, look at it good-naturedly and say, "Well, we have all there is to have—each one of us has twenty-four hours a day!" Part of the fact that life is a pilgrimage is that there never seems to be enough time to finish things. This can be very beautiful, if understood as part of the pilgrimage. However, right now I am thinking particularly of giving our time in such a way that others do not feel we are unwilling to wait for them, tapping our toes impatiently. We do not excoriate a child of seven for not being as tall as a child of twelve ought to be. We do not become enraged at a teenager for not yet being forty in understanding and experience. Yet often we are unwilling to wait for one another. Again there is a great paradox: the less we are willing to wait for a person to come to understanding and to grow, the more slowly will the person grow. The more we are willing to wait for that hour of fuller understanding to come, hastening it by our suffering love, then the faster the person will grow. It is a wonderful paradox.

We must also be engaged in the almsgiving of compassionate, suffering love. Often we fail to be compassionate because we don't see how anybody could have some particular problem. "How could she have that problem? I don't have it!" Since her problem is alien to my own experience, I am unwilling to reach out in suffering to try to understand something I do not personally know. This inhibits the other's growth and my own growth, as well. Maybe the other person is tempted to think, "How can she be so obtuse and unfeeling when all these little things cut me right to the heart?" You can multiply the examples unendingly. The closer we come to Jesus in our prayer and our penitence this Lent, the more we will be urged to that almsgiving of compassionate understanding, because he is the only one who understands everybody completely and thoroughly. Becoming compassionate, coming to understand one another, is the very opposite of condoning faults—the very opposite.

To these very particular forms of almsgiving, I add a fourth: the alms of good example. There is, perhaps, no alms more telling for the needy proud than to see the beauty of humility. There is nothing that can so impel one who has become party to small infidelities and little byways off the path of complete, pure obedience, than seeing the freshness and beauty of a completely obedient person to whom no fidelity is small, because each belongs to the greatness of giving. A truly humble person is always so beautiful. A completely obedient person is so engaging, so inviting. So let us give these alms to one another also, and find many more ways of almsgiving this Lent.

Saturday of the Fourth Week of Lent

Conversion

It seems only a few hours ago that we were approaching the fourth Sunday of Lent. As we approach the fifth Sunday of Lent, let us turn all the more deeply to consider the need for conversion. The fact that we have all undoubtedly missed some opportunities for conversion must not inspire in us any sense of fruitless defeat, but a new energy: I can't delay, because in no time at all we will be looking toward Passion Sunday.

Conversion is a most beautiful word. The Latin root is very obvious: *con* and *versare*, "to turn with"—as in a dance. Let us meditate on all that the art of ballet has to teach us in the spiritual life. Those who went to dance school were always taught about the turn, the *versus*. A good dancer was one who completed her turn, who did not begin brilliantly and then stagger at the end. I once read an article about a well-known ballerina that mentioned her brilliance as a dancer who completed her turns. The article spoke of another dancer and said, "She seemed to begin as a brilliant performer, but she does not complete her turns." This is conversion: to complete our turns. This is what we want to do in Lent. It is not that someday I'm going to do this, or that I make a halfhearted effort to do this. One can hardly think of anything more ludicrous than a halfhearted turn in the dance. There has to be enough energy to carry the dancer through the turn. So also during Lent, we want to make a full turn. There is nothing more unrewarding in the end than a halfhearted effort.

I looked at what the *Catechism of the Catholic Church* had to say about conversion:

> Conversion is accomplished in daily life by gestures of reconciliation, concern for the poor, the exercise and defense of Justice and right, by the admission of faults to one's brethren, fraternal correction, revision of life, examination of conscience, spiritual direction, acceptance of suffering, endurance of persecution for the sake of righteousness. Taking up one's cross each day and following Jesus is the surest way of penance (CCC 1435).

The *Catechism* encourages us to strive for conversion in daily life through gestures of reconciliation. How do we symbolically express our desire to repent and be reconciled with God and our neighbors? We strike our breast. We do this liturgically; we do this communally. But it is up to us how much meaning we put into this. When I strike my breast during the penitential rite at Mass, is it just a gesture or do I complete the turn of my thought, the *conversio*? Is my heart verbalizing in thought and in intent what this gesture is saying: that I want to turn around all the way?

A lovely gesture, frequent in the dance, is that the

danseur assists the ballerina to complete her turn as his hand beckons to her. This is what a community or family is: an assembly of one helping the other to complete turns in conversion, in holiness. How do we do this? In many ways: by a smile, by quick forgiveness, by an expression of understanding—not necessarily verbalized at all. This inspires the spiritual dancer to complete her turn. The heart bows before the mystery of another. What is perhaps a suffering for one is perhaps just a little annoyance or nothing at all for another, or vice versa. All of this pertains to conversion, that we turn enough in our own self-knowledge with the grace of God and the help of one another.

The next point the *Catechism* mentions is concern for the poor. We are are all poor in one way or another, and we know that everyone has downward pulls. Who does not make that great and sincere resolve, "I will never sin again; I will never commit a fault again; I will never do that again"? Christ-like love for one another should always be extricating one another from brambles and carrying the burden of another home to the fullness of herself in love and rejoicing. In a very lofty sense, a fault committed and humbly confessed is always something to rejoice about. It is related to the divine Shepherd carrying the wayward little sheep home on his shoulders.

The *Catechism* mentions confession of faults as another path to daily conversion. It is liberating to say, "There was something wrong here and I did it. I want you to know that I know that I did it. I want you to know that

I am sorry." No one ever went skulking off after a confession like that. You feel strengthened, you feel newly inspired, and everyone is relieved, beginning with yourself. So every confession of faults renews us, as telling the truth is invariably refreshing. It inspires us, it strengthens us, and it mellows us.

This leads us to revision of life. That is a wonderful word, isn't it? What is the real meaning of *revision*? "I see it again." Something that has become blurred to me, that I have glanced away from, I see again. I see it when I am penitential, when I have been quick to confess my faults and am very deeply sincere about this. Then I can revise my life, then I see all things with a clearer vision. I see them again, and they look different now: it wasn't that I didn't get my way in a situation, but that I missed an opportunity to let God have his way. A revision of life means to see it from a better angle, God's angle.

Anyone who writes anything always has to revise it. You have to go back and read it again. You always see something you can change for the better. If you write something, close the book, and send it to the printer, it will never be what it could have been if you had looked again, if you had revised it. A million times more must this be said of our spiritual life. We must be revising it always and changing it for the better. Even more than a writer of prose, a poet has to revise, revise. The great Francis Thompson would sit three hours by the side of the sea trying to find the right word, the right way to frame his thought. I don't advise you to spend that much time trying to get the right word, but seriously, we do not want to work less than the poet would. We must be doing this always in the spiritual life. It is a wonderful thing to look at our responses again and to see how much better they could be, how much more in tune with the Gospel. Let us learn from the arts of poetry and the dance how to put into practice what the *Catechism* tells us about conversion. Where are we not completing our turns? Where do we have to work harder?

FIFTH WEEK OF LENT

Fifth Sunday of Lent, Year A

The Stone Rolled Away

A FLEETING WEEK AGO we were much occupied with the joy of Laetare Sunday. This Sunday the Church wants us to be occupied with death. She is talking about graves, people in graves. Yet how does she present this to us? In the First Reading, we have Ezekiel talking to us about graves. He is talking about opening graves, not about digging them. He is talking about life coming forth from a grave. "I will open your graves", God says through the mouth of his prophet, "and have you rise from them" (Ezek 37:12, NAB). Then in Saint John's Gospel story of Lazarus (Jn 11:3–45) we find death, death in its beginning putrefaction, and out of it coming life. In the sentence of death pronounced by God upon our first parents and given as their dark legacy to all of us, there is from the beginning the promise of resurrection from death.

Now let us look at the details of these death stories of Ezekiel and John. Ezekiel is saying in God's stead, "I will open your graves and have you rise from them." From our experience of the grave and of human demise, we know that something must occur before life can arise from a grave. God is not saying to us through the prophet, "I will open your graves so that you may view your own putrefaction." But he says, "and have you rise from them." God did indeed impose upon us all the sentence of death, but it was by no means his final word.

Out of death comes rising. Even for the Mother of Jesus there may have been a brief taste of death before she came forth from the grave. Theologians are not agreed on whether or not she suffered death. Why would God let her die at all since she was excused from the consequences of death? Some say she had to experience everything but sin with us, even death. Her own Son died, and she would not want to be excused from what he had to suffer.

We might think these are two very separate categories of thought: on the one hand, the graves spoken of in Ezekiel and in John's Gospel; on the other, our Lady, preserved from all the effects of death and sin. But let us look at how she illumines these passages.

We look at that figure of Lazarus. It is vividly described for us. His hands are bound. His feet are bound. His face is masked. We see there clearly the picture of the spiritual death of sin, whether it is that fatal death of mortal sin or the paralysis of our venial sins, our faults. Our hands are bound, our feet are bound, and our vision is obscured. As we look to our Lady, to Lazarus, and back again, we see that her hands were always open. What is the significance for us in the bound hands of Lazarus when we are thinking of spiritual death or spiritual malaise? These are hands no longer able to give. Whenever we fail to give our love, our service to others, then our hands are bound. Our Lady's never were. They were always open, always giving. She was completely alive, which perhaps can be described as a state of always giving. Her hands were open to serve, to cradle, to comfort all of her multitudinous children, along with her Divine Child. They are open still. They did not close in that brief second of her human death, but are always open.

At the beginning of this episode when Lazarus was ill, Jesus said to the apostles, "This sickness will not end in death." When little sicknesses (and they can seem very large) come upon us spiritually, they never end in death unless we ourselves tie our hands and our feet and veil our faces from the vision.

Lazarus' hands and feet had to be untied. We can picture the scene easily: people were staring openmouthed in stupefaction. He must have been quite a figure because he could only hobble. He could not walk with those bound feet. He could not see. To show that it was not just a ghostly phenomenon that their excited minds were projecting on reality, our Lord asked that he be untied so that he could again do what hands are supposed to do: to reach out, to clasp, to give, to serve.

What ties us in spiritual death? What binds our hands? We know it is selfishness. We know that sloth, laziness, unwillingness to serve, tie our hands because hands are made to be outstretched. Continuing our considerations from yesterday on the dancer, we know that no ballerina can perform with bound hands. Can you imagine anything as preposterous as a beautiful dancer executing lovely steps with her hands bound, her hands clenched together? In the dance, the hands lead while the feet always follow the hands. And so one might say the initial beauty in the dancer is in her open hands. How much more in the spiritual dancer! You cannot serve with bound hands, you cannot dance with bound hands. A closed hand is for holding on to something for yourself, for striking. A fist is the exact opposite of giving and serving and embracing and soothing, everything that a hand is meant to do.

Then we look at the feet. When are our feet bound? When they are no longer running to serve; when they are no longer hastening swiftly on the path to God, on the way of service, but are bound by sloth, by selfishness. The dancer's feet follow the hands and then the whole body follows the leadership of the extremities. So spiritually does the soul, the heart, follow the outreach of giving and the quickness of moving to serve. Our Lady's feet were never bound. They were always going along the way of service. She had open hands; she had hurrying feet.

Then we consider the face: Lazarus could not see; he was dead. When we do not see the needs of others, when we are not occupied with looking upon the needs of the Church and the suffering world, then, too, our face is covered over in the imprisonment of ourselves. Our Lady had a sweeping vision. She had an open visage with smiles and tears to share with others, to encourage them and unite them with one another.

It would be very profitable to ponder her brief appearances in the Gospels and to ask whether she was smiling at certain moments. Surely at the wedding of Cana after she had made her appeal to her Divine Son and the miracle was performed, she must have been smiling. Surely her shining face must have said in the loveliest way, "See? You see what he can do?" or even, "See what he can do when I ask him?" Her face was always so open, often smiling, sometimes weeping, sometimes suffering, sometimes jubilant. Lazarus' face had to be released from what covered his vision and made it impossible for him to speak, and impossible for anyone to see Lazarus' smile. Was this not perhaps the first thing that Lazarus did when he was restored to life and the cloth was removed from his face: smile at our Lord? I think it must have been. Their eyes met, and he smiled at Jesus.

We can get into a habit of walking in darkness, which is not walking at all. We can do this by becoming judgmental, suspicious, complaining, querulous. We can get into a habit of a closed fist instead of an open hand, of bound feet instead of a swift-serving gait. The most complaining people, and I do not think there is ever an exception to this, are inevitably those who give the least. This is what it is to have bound feet.

What does the stone mean? Our dear Lord had to say, "Roll away the stone", before he could even release the hands and the feet and uncover the visage. Is not the stone a preference for the selfishness that seeks to justify the closed hand and the indolent feet and the petulant, frowning visage? It would be good for us to find the stone that tends to roll into place, or that we ourselves roll into place at the great aperture of our lives, where life and love should flow out from us upon our community and the Church and the world.

Ezekiel says, "I will open your graves and and have you rise from them . . . I will put my spirit in you that you may live." This is not a dour Sunday liturgy. It is joyous. It is well placed after Laetare; there is a rolling away of the stone so that at Easter we come forth into new life, an unbinding of the hands to give and to soothe, an untying of the feet for generous service, an opening of the face to light. I must say I love to think of Lazarus smiling at our Lord. A smile is a sign of life. A frown is always in a certain way a sign of death. A wrinkled, dark visage is a portent of death. Something is not alive in the heart. Something is dying. Something is sick in the heart when the visage is clouded over.

Let us also consider Martha as she makes her act of faith with a bit of loving reproach in it: "Lord, if you had been here, my brother would not have died." She is not exactly ready to say, "Where were you?" But she is close enough to him to make her little loving complaint, and then to submerge it in a great act of faith: "Even now I know that whatever you ask of God, God will give you." When we experience certain deaths within ourselves, it is because we are not allowing the full presence of Christ to live there. We can say to him, "If I had given you full freedom in my life, I would not have died that bad death yesterday, this one today. I would not have this loss of spiritual vision. I would not have these ungiving hands. I would not have these selfish, unmoving feet." If we are in the company of Jesus, we can and we must suffer, but we do not spiritually die. We even have that expression, "Oh, I'm just tied up in knots." It is a very apt expression. Life is not flowing in me. When we are tied up in knots, we always know who tied them: we did.

It is wonderful to picture this event, to try to hear that cry of our Lord in our hearts: "Come forth!" It must have been electrifying for those who were there. He must have said it in a loud, imperious voice, the voice of One who has the power to command, who is in charge of life and of death—a presage of the great Day of Judgment, when we shall all rise from the grave. In these last two precious weeks of Lent, our dear Lord will be saying to us again and again, "Come forth, come forth." Only if we rise, as we surely want to do, and start stumbling forward in our clumsiness, the result of our many faults, will he then untie the feet and the hands, and clear the vision. When he has perfected that work in us, as we will allow him, then what will happen? It will be Easter. Amen.

Fifth Sunday of Lent, Year B

❧

Scholarship

In the Gospel for today's liturgy we hear our Lord speaking to us very seriously about what is to come upon him. Before that, the Second Reading from Hebrews proclaims that heart-shaking, soul-shaking, mind-shaking word about Jesus, "Son though he was, he learned obedience from what he suffered" (Heb 5:8, NAB). He learned it, as a man, through suffering. There is no other way to learn it. Truly in the spiritual life there is nothing that we can learn without some form of suffering.

Let us think for a few minutes about the process of learning. All real learning requires a great effort. Sometimes we say of a very bright child, "Oh, he learns so easily." This is not precisely true. He may grasp principles. He may be able to draw conclusions with more alacrity than some of his companions, but real learning always requires effort. One could perhaps define the greatest scholars as those who have put forth the most effort with the equipment that God gave them. There is always some form of suffering in all learning because there must be patience, and patience is suffering. There is always humility in learning. It is the great scholars who realize how little they know. We see that in every age.

Looking back on the great scholarship of the past, we remember the so-familiar words of the great Saint Thomas Aquinas, surely one of God's masterpieces of an intellectual saint: "All that I have written is like a little straw." And he spoke correctly. Before the omniscience of God, the products of the greatest thinker are like a little straw —albeit very precious straw. He was so brilliant spiritually that he knew that. It is the so-called theologians of our time who do not think that what they are writing or saying is a little straw. They think it is the great new message for the world. They speak from a height, whereas the truly great ones always speak from a depth, on their knees, prostrate before God.

The great scholars are those who realize how very little they know. In science or the arts, when one is learning more and more, perhaps one is most of all learning how little one knows. Indeed what Alexander Pope said comes to mind, "A little learning is a dangerous thing", unless it drives us on to more. So there is always suffering effort in learning; there is always patience; there is always the need for humility. I have to realize how much I do not know in order to be able to learn. It would be a strange student who went to high school or even to the university and who said, "I know the field; I have nothing more to learn."

When the great Dr. Robert Hutchins was teaching at

the University of Chicago, students were crowding into the classes of this great pedagogue. He gave an assignment, and he came back next day and asked, "Now, what are your questions?" They were waiting for him to pour knowledge into them. And so he repeated, "Ladies and gentlemen, what are your questions?" They looked at him in silence. He said, "Well, good morning, ladies and gentlemen", and he left. Then he came the second day and he did the same thing. They began thinking how much they were paying for this course, and asked the meaning of his strange behavior. He said, "Ladies and gentlemen, if you have no questions, then you must know as much about it as I do. I have nothing to say." We are real learners, real students when we realize how much we don't know, and most of all in the spiritual life.

Real learning brings us to greater and greater depth, a greater understanding of God within our poor little human limitations, and a greater understanding of ourselves. We have only a superficial understanding of ourselves. It can never be complete, because God knows that we aren't quite able to take ourselves in a single great gulp. He said to his apostles, "I have yet many things to say to you, but you cannot bear them now" (Jn 16:12). He told them little by little, and they went on learning. We smile with gratitude and understanding as we read the Gospels, to see how they advanced rather slowly. They advanced from the same depths of nonunderstanding that we experience in ourselves. We tend to linger in a circumstance or happening or suffering, not allowing God show it to us as part of a great whole.

Learning in the spiritual life requires great effort. The Son of God, as man, had to learn obedience in the only way that the depths of virtue are ever learned, in suffering, waiting in patience for the parts to express a whole. In Jesus' human life, all of what we may dare to call the everyday sufferings—the denseness of his disciples (sometimes they seem almost as dense as we are), the effrontery of so many around him, the ingratitude he found on every side—all of this led him humanly toward the great mystery of suffering patience consummated in his Passion and his death. Our little minds have to grapple with these thoughts because they are great and they require effort for us to try to assimilate their profound depths of meaning. Through suffering, he learned as man to obey the will of the Father. Every suffering on the human level made him, already the wisest of men, wiser yet. Let me say that again because it means very much to me. On the human level, as a man, the most perfect of all creatures, he had to wrestle with the knowledge of each circumstance, each suffering that came into his life, one after another, to come to the summit of suffering, which was absolute self-giving in the Passion and in his death.

In earthly scholarship we see how real students have to persevere in effort. They have to begin at the beginning and often have to return to the beginning. Much more spiritually do we have to begin at the beginning and keep returning to the beginning. There is no higher mathematics or mathematical science that can ever be achieved without knowing our multiplication tables. No great mathematician begins by saying, "That's kid's stuff. I'm going to be a great, great mathematician." Great scholars begin with the multiplication tables, which they and we, as children, rattled off for our teacher or an insistent parent. There is no memorization on the human plane without effort.

There has never been any scholarship that did not involve both drudgery and exhilaration, and this is a thousand times more true in the spiritual life. Sometimes, let's face it, it feels like drudgery. We are plodding on and on, and we fall down again and again, and it seems we are not getting anywhere. But then there comes a day, a time when we have a new little spark of understanding. When we study the lives of great men, we see this. They studied and they pondered and they wondered and they considered and they studied some more. Then there came moments of understanding, of highest exhilaration, when they understood. Some scientists have literally run around with exhilaration. They have thrown their hands in the air and said, "Eureka! Now I understand! I understand!" We should not deny ourselves spiritually those moments of exhilaration. We need to remember that these moments are never reached without what I dare to call the spiritual drudgery of every day and the dreary little things that are continually going wrong. So often we find ourselves back at "A". This will always be the case, in some sense. If only we realize that, yes, we are back at "A" and don't insist that we are at "C", there can come a moment of exhilaration.

Then there is a last point: the recognition of limitations. The greatest scholars are those who best know their limitations. The ones who know very little are the ones who say they know it all. So we need a recognition of limitations. Hopefully the older we grow, the more we realize our limitations and see, "My goodness, I should have grasped that a long time ago. I should have known how I should have reacted in this circumstance and did not. I know how I should have accepted that and did not." Maybe that is not a star-encrusted moment of Joy, but recognition of limitations is a very great thing. It is a step forward.

Out of these considerations we discover things in ourselves and in our relations with others. We all know we more easily excuse faults in a person full of faults than in one who may excel spiritually in many ways. We are surprised, we are saddened when we see something untoward in someone from whom we expected much better than this. This experience is part of God's image in us. When he sees us, as he does, full of faults and calling them by their right names, he can, so to speak, more easily excuse us.

The second point is that we are more surprised and amazed at the mistake of the master musician than by the blunders of the less gifted. I think that is very heartening in our spiritual life. When someone is just beginning in a field, or perhaps is not extraordinarily gifted in a field, we want to cover up the blunder. We are eager to express appreciation of each little step forward. God is the same way. When we frequently play the wrong notes (and we hear it, too), then he is quick to cover over our blunder. But if we think that we are before God with a master's degree in the spiritual life, it is not as easy for God to find excuses for us. If we insist that we are right, what can God do?

I hope I have been able to put together what is clear in my own heart and which in some way leads to that wonderful saying of Saint Athanasius, "How fine a thing it is to move from feast to feast." It is a feast to know where we are wrong, where we have failed to use God's grace, failed to rise to an occasion. That is moving from feast to feast because we are becoming more humble. I think that God cries out, "How fine a thing!" We should cry out, "How fine a thing it was! A wrong note and I heard it. It was a sour chord and I heard it." How fine a thing it is to move from this, and from holy day to holy day. For the grace of the feast of Easter, of what it means to rise from the dead in our daily lives, is always at hand, as Saint Athanasius says, to enlighten the minds that desire it.

I ask you to draw these thoughts together. If Christ learned obedience through suffering, then we will not learn it any other way, and the same with all of the virtues. We will only learn what humility is by suffering through our pride and calling it by its right name. We shall only learn full self-giving by recognizing our self-centeredness and our selfishness, and calling them by their right names. These are very encouraging thoughts. I hope that in these last two weeks of Lent we will advance in learning, learn more by using the little sufferings of every day, and be more learned by the end of this Lent.

Fifth Sunday of Lent, Year C

Pushing On

Now we come to the the solemn weeks of Passiontide. Swiftly, swiftly go the days, and in this final stretch of Lent the devil is very busy. He gets busier and busier. The Gospel of the first Sunday said that the devil left our dear Lord "until an opportune time" (Lk 4:13). The devil is full of diabolical zeal to push on quickly to what he wants to have. What does he want? It is that we should be despondent, that we should feel, "Oh, what is the use?" after all the misspent graces of this Lent, all the things that seem to be going wrong. Knowing that, God inspired the Apostle to exhort us in today's Second Reading to strain forward. I like the old translation which said "push on" (see Phil 3:13). Not "walk on" or "run on", but *push*, which means to put the things that are in your way out of the way. Let us in our meditation and our prayer this coming week see what we need to push out of the way.

What is impeding our swiftly moving toward a deeper union with our crucified Lord than ever before? What do we need to push out of the way? It is usually not polite to push people or things out of our way. But spiritually that is what I should do when the interior obstacles of my faults are impeding me from moving swiftly: give them one good push that will send them reeling. There is just *one* person to whom I need to give a good push—myself and my attachment to myself. Let's be very "pushy" in this week. We do not usually use that colloquial word in a very pleasant way; but in the way I am speaking now, out of the love and the eagerness of my heart, it is different. In this way it is wonderful to be really "pushy".

Isaiah is telling us that we are a people that God formed for himself so that we might announce his praise (see Is 43:21). When, with the strength of grace, we have pushed out of our way what does not belong there, what impedes our progress into the heart of Jesus, then we can each of us be the person that he formed for himself to announce his praise. We can announce it in so many ways to one another. Every act of virtue, every smile, every act of love, every act of mercy and forgiveness announces his praise, because it is all due to him. We can do nothing good of ourselves. But "I can do all things in him who strengthens me" (Phil 4:13). Every good thing that I allow his grace to achieve in me announces his praise.

I announce his praise and show what his mercy can achieve, what his grace can do, by my humility and my thankfulness in being forgiven, my joy in being allowed to go on living, my wonder that God has not wiped me out yet! God has not given up on me.

Again in Philippians, Saint Paul tells us "to know him and the power of his resurrection and [the] sharing of his sufferings by being conformed to his death" (Phil 3:10,

NAB); or, in another translation, "by being formed into the pattern of his death". His death leads to his Resurrection, and our own little deaths united with his can lead to our resurrection. We have to be formed in that pattern of his death and rising. What is that pattern? It is a pattern that keeps repeating the motif. He forgives, and then he forgives again. He shows mercy, and then he shows mercy again and again. He places his hope in us, and, despite all our counter-evidence, he hopes and hopes again. Despite our poor response to his love, he loves and loves again, on and on and on. This is his pattern. We can only push on in his pattern of death and rising, that pattern of mercy, of forgiving, of hoping, and of loving.

Monday of the Fifth Week of Lent

Going Another Way

Today we read the Gospel about the woman caught in adultery, a story we know very well, but the meaning of which we can never ponder deeply enough. Our Lord tells the woman, "Go, [and] from now on do not sin any more" (Jn 8:11, NAB). He was urging her to avoid this sin, to go another way. We recall that the Magi returned to their home by another way (see Mt 2:12). They knew it was not a wise course to return to this insanely ambitious king with the news they had to bring. What would happen? Would he kill them? Very likely. Would there be a terrible uproar? Indeed. And so they went back by another way.

In a more profound spiritual sense, we must go back another way. If my greatest weakness is this or that or the other thing, then our Lord is saying to me as well as to the woman, "Avoid this. Don't get near it." If, for instance, my weakness is a brooding that makes me morose, makes me complain, makes me blame others and excuse myself, then I must avoid it. If I sit down and talk with this, whatever it is, something wrong is bound to happen.

It is the human will we are talking about. We know we sin only with the will. This is the greatest of our faculties. It is the sovereign power, the one that decides. Nonwilling is also an act of the will. We will to do this, or we will not to do this. We decide. To do a good thing unwillingly has no worth whatsoever because it is not done with the consent of the will. I will to look at what I have done wrong and call it by its right name. I will to receive this correction. I will to be faithful. There is the whole merit. To do what of itself is a good thing unwillingly is simply an outward observance, for a real act of the will is never the result of coercion. The will cannot be coerced. The will is served or disserved by the inferior faculties. It can be approached by the imagination. It can be almost engaged in battle with memory, but it cannot be coerced. It can be drawn, it can be persuaded, but it cannot be forced. The sovereign power makes its sovereign decision. When deciding to do what is right and to forget what is not worth remembering, the will is sometimes bruised and beleaguered but still goes forward to all that is worth doing.

So a human act pertains only to the will. The will can be assaulted, the will can be tempted, the will can sometimes be almost tortured by the passions, by the senses, by the imagination, by the memory of a hurt, by the memory of a wrong. But real consent belongs only to the will. Our Lord is saying, "Make a sovereign act of the will to avoid this." He is saying, "Be unwilling to do this." We can be very drawn to something, likely enough in our weakness, and find it engaging. Sometimes the most unengaging things can seem so engaging. Why not be morose? Why not go over and over the hurt? Or go over and over what you think is a wrong? But to be unwilling to do this, ah—that is a different thing.

We want to make a firm resolve, "Yes, in the future I am going to avoid this particular avenue of thought, where I know I will get into trouble; this particular lane of imagination, this particular little byway of memory, which will not bring me into closer union with Jesus and his sufferings. I will avoid this."

Tuesday of the Fifth Week of Lent

Right Complaining

In today's First Reading, we see the Israelites complaining (Num 21:4–9). Ordinarily we think of a complaint as something peevish, querulous; and that is indeed a meaning of the word, but it has another sense. To complain is to grieve, to bewail. We have this often in the Scriptures where the psalmist is asking God to pay attention while he wails and grieves. "Hear my voice, O God, in my complaint" (Ps 64:1). This has nothing to do with grumbling, with wanting to put suffering out of the way.

Complain is from the Latin verb *plangere*, which means, "to wound, to strike". It means in a very particular way, "to strike the breast". This is the way to complain. In this sense, may we all be great complainers during Lent, striking our breast again and again as God unfolds to us his graces and illumines us more and more with his light, so that we are more and more inclined to say, "O God, be merciful to me, a sinner."

There is a wonderful way to complain, which is to grieve that God is not loved, that God is not glorified. We find Saint Francis spending the whole night wandering in misery through the woods complaining, "Love is not loved", a very pure, spiritual complaint—a grieving, a bewailing. This should be the great complaint of the contemplative: that God is not glorified, God is not loved, God is not thanked, God is not responded to. I grieve in my heart, and I bewail this. This kind of complaint is a very positive thing. It drives me to glorify him. It drives me to love him. It drives me to try to refuse him nothing. This is a wonderful way to complain.

But unfortunately, there is the other type of complaint. We want suffering put out of the way. "This is not right. It should be changed; it should be expunged from the roster. It should be taken right off of the agenda of my life." But this is God's agenda. I want to do only the will of God, but somebody upset my plans. Yes, I want to get to Easter, but not by suffering anything. I do not want anybody to try my patience. But Jesus was patient unto death, Jesus was patient with churls, Jesus is patient with me.

Lent is the time, as the younger generation would say, to "smarten up", and not to act as though we have no faith in the spiritual life at all. We can either be grateful for the rainfall or complain because the weeds then grow faster. We can be grateful for the beauty of the snow, or we can complain because it gets dirty after a while. We can be grateful that it falls, or complain because we have to shovel it up. We can complain about anything, even the most beautiful things.

This is the season to drop peevishness and to enter into the kind of complaining that Saint Francis did: "Love is not loved", and I will love him. God is not glorified, and I must be driven to glorify him. I must be panting for little secret offerings to make to him: the offended glance that I will not give, the turning away that I will not do, the smile I will give when I want to frown. The days are so rich with them. They are on every side. God has such a wonderful plan for each one of us. He wants to prepare us to rise out of all our miseries, but we cannot rise out of them without dyings. These are beautiful dyings. So let us allow God to bring us out of that querulous complaining and grumbling, the insistence that anything that irritates or troubles me must be changed. If with God's grace we put that aside, then we enter into this beautiful *plangere*, "to strike the breast, to be stricken". That is a very wonderful thing.

Charity is the absolute Gospel value. Everything is subservient to that. Love is the answer to everything. When we do not return love in situations that are difficult, no wonder we are lacking in Gospel answers. Love *is* the answer. Sometimes we do not want to take a situation or another's burden upon ourselves. We want to get rid of it. But Jesus took upon himself the burdens of us all.

Let us face ourselves, not miserably but determinedly with these facts, and choose what kind of complainers we are going to be. We know the choice we want to make, but we have to work hard at it because it is a choice born of God, and therefore requires much effort and much prayer. The other possible choices are born of sinful, fallen human nature and require no effort whatsoever. Let us be the right kind of complainers.

Wednesday of the Fifth Week of Lent

The Work of Salvation

In the Passion account of Saint Luke, Jesus predicts to Peter that he will fall hard after his boasting. But he says, "I have prayed for you that your own faith may not fail; and once you have turned again, strengthen your brethren" (Lk 22:32). We have failed so many times. We have boasted, half-innocently, about the fidelity we were going to show. We would never fail him again, and we have fallen. But he says to us, too, "Once you have turned back again, strengthen your brethren." God always works to save, and when we have recovered, then we save others. The work of a community or family is to be always saving one another. We know that *to save* means "to make whole, to make healthy". God works to heal us, laboring at this as any dedicated doctor works to make the sick one well. Then when the sick one has recovered, he is to go out and give strength to others.

In Jesus' life before the days of his sacred Passion, we see him continually working to save. He was working to save situations. He was working to save people's reputations. He was working to restore persons, working to restore integrity, working to save this one's dignity, to save this other one from embarrassment.

We see him at his first public appearance doing something to save the situation, working the miracle of changing water into wine, which might seem to us not worth doing (see Jn 2:1–11). Perhaps this was not the miracle we would have chosen as an appropriate first miracle—just to save a young couple from embarrassment. But we are called in our own way to work this miracle of saving. How often has this day's wine run out? Maybe someone in this circumstance or this situation has no wine left, but only bitter waters of discouragement, turgid waters of impatience, troubled waters of irritability. Her wine is very low, and we are called with our love to work this miracle for her, to bring our love to change her poor water into wine. Then, the day will come for the worker of this miracle of love when this situation is reversed and she is the one with some bitter water. Sometimes a person's own depths have been disturbed by temptation, by suffering, by affliction, and her waters are clouded. Someone comes with the miracle of love to change the water into the wine of love. Then, as I say, this same miracle will be returned to us. In the mystery of community we have one another to save the situation, to save one another, not to be upset by turgid waters.

We see Jesus filled with loyalty toward the woman who was accused of extravagance (see Mt 26:8). Why was she pouring this perfume so lavishly over him? The small-minded took issue with the extravagance of her loyalty. Jesus never merely meets loyalty with loyalty, but he infinitely surpasses it. The world would say this woman was foolish for spending everything she had on him in one great burst. Jesus returned her loyal love with the loyalty of prophecy: "Truly, I say to you, wherever this gospel is preached in the whole world, what she has done will be told, in memory of her" (Mt 26:13). He made her little extravagance, judged imprudent by the world, famous to the end of time. He worked to save and to glorify the loyalty of her who thought that it is a very good use of one's life to pour it out over him, not to do anything worldly-wise, but just to throw oneself away on him. He also worked to save those who were critical of her and whose understanding was so limited.

We find him again and again working to save. We think of the apostles on the road with him, squabbling about who is going to be greater, who will be the leader, who will be the outstanding one. We find him saving their poor, tattered dignity not by accusing them, but by giving them an opportunity to rise out of this. He asked them a question, "What were you talking about?" He was working to save them, not by condemnation but by inviting them to confrontation with the truth. By enticing them to confess their fault, he was working to save.

We can go through the whole Gospel and see him again and again working to save the situation, to save tattered dignity, to save an embarrassed person. We see how we are called to do all of these things in community. We see him with the crowd which is about to faint with hunger, and he has almost no supplies. He works to save them from infirmity, from fainting on the way (see Mk 8:1–9). This is our call in community. We too can work this miracle. Each of us has only a little bit to give, only our limited self; but if it is totally given, it will never be spent. When we give this small loaf of our energy, of our love, of our caring, we will discover there is another loaf to give and another and another until the last day of our life comes. We are called in community to keep multiplying our love, our strength, our energy so that no one faints on the way, so that every other one is strengthened by each one's giving. He worked to save us. He worked miracles, and we are called to work miracles of love. Love is always a miracle.

Let us thank God that he worked to save us, that Jesus worked so hard to save us, and that it was not only in the Agony in the Garden, it was not only at the scourging, it was not only at the crowning with thorns, it was not only in the bitter mockery and the indescribable contempt, it was not only hanging on the Cross that he worked to save us. I could dare to say he had been practicing for his Passion all of his life, always working to save us. We are called to work to save, and we can never allow ourselves to think that salvation, spiritual health, is ever achieved without work. Let us work together.

Thursday of the Fifth Week of Lent

❧

Life-Giving Repentance

On the feast of the Chair of Saint Peter we heard the story in the Acts of the Apostles in which Saint Peter recalls the events that led him to make the decisions he made (see Acts 11:4–18). His companions were not very happy with the decisions he was making and felt free (which is beautiful to observe) to question him about this. Saint Peter recalls to them the whole vision he had with its very moving, mystical aspects and its humorously human aspects. We remember the food being lowered in a cloth and Saint Peter being told to eat and how he said he would never do this. He was very faithful to the law. He protested, "Far be this thing from me." Then we have this delightful response of God to him: "Don't you call unclean what I have blessed." So Saint Peter converted.

He explains all this to his little company, and they listen. They are able to hear, and as a result they praise God that life-giving repentance has been given to the Gentiles. This is a great gift of God: to be able to repent. We need to remember this when, particularly as Lent comes to its end, we are appalled at the heap of things for which we need to repent. But we would not even know that we had any need of repentance without a gift of God. To want to repent, to be sorry, is a gift of God for which we must be very grateful. It is a great thing to be given the sense to repent, the sense to know that we are wrong. That is part of the mystery of Joyful penitence. At least I can do this: with God's grace I can hear the sour notes. I see the wreckage and I want to repent.

This gift is described as life-giving. This is at the heart of the Lenten mystery and is the reason why it is a joyous season. The more we repent, the more alive we are. The more we lack the sight of how much we need to repent, the less alive we are. I suppose one could conclude that the only way to be thoroughly and irrevocably dead spiritually is not to see a need for repentance.

Those who listen to God are able to hear what he is saying, to convert; and they come alive with repentance. Repentance is such an energetic thing, an energizing thing. When we fall into lassitude or spiritual torpor or sit down in the mud puddle of our mood or our dejection, inevitably we have not listened to the grace of God within us so that the life-giving urge of repentance is not there. But the more repentant we are, the more alive we are.

Then, in today's Gospel our dear Lord, as the Second Person of the triune God, says to the Jews, "Before Abraham was, I AM" (Jn 8:58). Of course they want to stone him; they want to get rid of him, because they understand what he is saying. Only God is essential Being *per se*. Our little being is utterly, completely contingent upon his essential Being. If God for one moment ceased to sustain us, to sustain our contingency on his Being, it is not that we would die, it is that we would cease to be. This room would be empty—not full of corpses—it would be empty. There wouldn't be anything here. But he sustains our contingency by his Being. He revealed the expression of that Being to us in response to Moses: "Say this to the sons of Israel: 'I AM has sent me to you'" (Ex 3:13, 14).

I was struck by this in a new way—since our being is contingent on the Divine Being, then the more I am alive in the love of God, in the grace of God, the more I am living my *I am*. Sometimes we use that phrase as an excuse: "Well, I'm just a moody person, that's the way I am. I am just an impatient, irascible person." We know what is meant, but never before did I understand that this is, so to speak, a blasphemy because *I am* is an expression of my little but gloriously contingent being. When I say, "That's just the way I am", this is a destructive element in my *I am*-ness. I hope I can convey to you how deeply this moved me when God put it into my heart and my mind. All the words of the Gospel are calling each of us to the fullness of her *I am*. Each wandering, each excuse takes on something akin to blasphemy because when we say, "That's the way I am", that's not my *I am*. That is everything my *I am* is not. I want to be conscious of the full dignity of my being, which is totally contingent on the essential Being of I AM.

In the beginning God looked upon all the works of his hands and "saw that it was good" (Gen 1:21). We love and relish the expression of the Scriptures that gives us such an image of God's tenderness in making man like a little clay doll (see Gen 2:7). It is as though God were holding all of this in the palm of his hand. All of our little *I am*s are there in the hand of God, and we are very good.

Every time we fulfill the work of God's hands that is each of us, we are proclaiming the name of God, and we are then reflecting the Being of God. Let us be very conscious of our dignity as little *I am*s struck off God, so that we can demand of ourselves that we more truly be reflections of God, sparks struck off his essential Being, that we glorify and proclaim and acclaim him throughout the Church, throughout the world, throughout the ages. God said to Moses, "Man shall not see me and live . . . you shall see my back; but my face shall not be seen" (Ex 33:20, 23). In a certain way we can say that we are like the back of God, and others must be able to see a reflection of the great I AM-ness of God in us.

Friday of the Fifth Week of Lent

A Full Sweep of Vision

WE ARE APPROACHING the end of Lent properly speaking, because Holy Week is an entity unto itself. Surely in all of us there is a great sense of expectancy. We prepare to enter into this holiest of weeks and we look back. It is necessary and important that we look back, even as we look forward into Holy Week and the Resurrection.

There are different ways in which we can look back, and many of them are wrong. The first way, which I think can be very tempting to us, is a kind of despair. We started out, surely all of us, with such high spiritual ambitions, and we fell. As we look back, a kind of despair can come over us. "Oh, what's the use? Another Lent and I have fallen and fallen again, and there were the same dreary faults succumbed to more than once." This is wrong.

There is a second way, the way of negative regret which says, "If only, if only I had responded to the opportunities, to the intimations of God's desires." This could sound humble, but it is not. It is also wrong.

Then there is a third way of looking back, which is almost the opposite of these, and that is a kind of phlegmatic way. "Oh, well, we are only human. We are all fallen people, and God expects us to commit faults; and, yes, there were a lot of things I did not respond to, but that is our poor humanity. That is the way it is, nothing to get discouraged about." And that is wrong.

The final way, related to the first, is a melancholy that can descend like a fog on the soul and on the heart. "Oh, it's too late. It's all over. We've come to the end of Lent." It is as though we were sitting down by a swamp and breathing in those poisonous airs that arise from it.

Then there are the four opposite ways of these. In place of the despair that says, "Oh, what is the use?" I can say instead, "There is yet time; there is yet hope. Am I not still alive? Is it not true that God has not struck me down? I somehow have to make it up to him."

Negative regret can be supplanted by the love that mends misused materials. It doesn't just throw them away and say, "Ruined, ruined, ruined!" But it mends. Love of God, not vanity, sees the stains on our behavior and washes them out. Love mends, love purges, love washes.

For the phlegmatic vision which says, "Oh well, I'm only human. We are all fallen people", we bring the healthy sense of shame. It is a very different thing to have a sense that I am so ashamed of myself, of the opportunities I have wasted, the graces I have not used. This is not debilitating, but healthy.

Then instead of melancholy we need invincible hope in Christ, invincible hope in God, who never gives up on us. The first four can look like humility but are so false. The second four are what is true.

The hymn at Vespers, "Audi, Benigne Conditor", shows us how God looks at things. We begin that hymn as sinners, with such confidence. The first word we say to God is "Listen". Then we remind God who he is: *benigne Conditor*. "You are a kind Maker, a kind Creator." A really kind Creator never gives up on his creation. The hymn goes on to say that we bring him "our prayers with tears in this sacred time of fasting, these forty days". In my favorite verse, we call him again by his name: *Scrutator alme cordium*, "kind reader of hearts". We know we are not always very kind in the way we estimate happenings, the way we judge things, the way we look into things. We sometimes are not kind in our scrutiny, but he is. How wonderful that the One who reads our hearts and knows everything in them, every dingy little corner and every spiritual cobweb, is kind. Then we tell him that he knows about the weakness of men: *Infirma tu scis virium*. "You know about it. And so we turn to you for the grace of forgiveness." *Remissiónis* is a wonderful word that means "forgiveness", in the sense of, "push it all away, do away with it".

What we want is a right vision, a full sweep of vision that there is yet time, that love mends, that shame is a healthy thing, and that invincible hope is found in Christ.

Expediency

As we stand on the threshold of Holy Week, we want to remind ourselves that each time we respond in fidelity to obedience, each time we humble ourselves, each time we show love, each time we are kind, we are renewing the Church. The greatest acts of fidelity are the silent ones. We must never allow ourselves to underestimate the value of those supposedly small acts of fidelity. Each time we unite ourselves to the meek and humble Jesus in the way that we respond, in our manner, our countenances, our words, our ready and joyous submission, every one of these most hidden acts is renewing the Church.

We know we cannot renew the Church without renewing one another. By every good act, whether hidden or overt, we renew others. There is nothing like the force of example. Nothing draws us toward humility like seeing the beauty of a humble person, the beauty of a humble response, the beauty of a humble word. Nothing more impresses upon us the beauty of recollection than observing it in one another.

In our day Christ is suffering much, both from members of his Church and those outside of it. By humble, silent fidelity, we are in our measure trying to heal these wounds that Christ receives. He must not be wounded by us. Let us take this deeply into our hearts. Where are we going in Holy Week? To heal the wounds of Christ in his Mystical Body, the wounds we too have inflicted on him.

When I pray the Way of the Cross, it always strikes me at the First Station that Jesus stood there silent when he was brought to trial. The Latin verb is in the imperfect tense, which indicates a continuing action. The Gospel does not say, "*Jesus tacuit*", but, "*Jesus tacebat*", which is literally "Jesus kept on being silent" (see Mt 26:63). Jesus kept on being silent all through the Passion. He went on. He had to go on avoiding the things that disturbed his human emotions. And so for ourselves it has to be *"Ego tacebo."* I will go on keeping silence. I will not enter into prolonged conversations with my difficulties and what I think are my little crosses—because the trouble with getting into these prolonged conversations is that we forget that crosses are meant to be carried, not dragged, and still less analyzed, studied, dissected, or judged. If so wonderful a thing should ever happen that we are blamed for something that we did not do, then let us rejoice and be glad because in that small measure we are one with Christ, who could never be justly blamed or accused of anything wrong.

Then, I would like to share a second thought from this morning's Gospel, in which Caiaphas said, "You know nothing at all, nor do you take into account that it is expedient for you that one man die for the people, and that the whole nation not perish" (Jn 11:49–50). He did not know how true was the word that he said. It was indeed terrible in the way that he said it, but it had a profound truth of which he was not aware. What does this phrase mean, "to be expedient"? Expediency is the use of methods that bring the most immediate benefits. Something which is expedient is conducive toward an end that is sought after, that is much desired. So indeed it was advantageous that this one man should die. His death was the greatest advantage that has ever been, the redemption of all mankind. Caiaphas, although he did not know it, was a prophet. It *was* expedient that this God-Man should die for the people.

It is also expedient that we should suffer many little interior dyings—to our willfulness, our self-indulgence, our vanity, all of that dreary litany that we know so well. It is expedient that these faults should be put to death. It is expedient for the Church of God. It is expedient for God's desire for the ongoing salvation of men. He has entrusted to us a sharing in the salvation of men. It is expedient that we should die for this.

So this is a little orientation toward Holy Week that I offer to you out of my own prayer, my own heart. Take it and blend it in with your own inspirations, your own prayer. May this week be, by our manner of living and our silent fidelity, a week of great renewal for the Church, during which we may prove before God how it is indeed expedient that each one of us should die for the salvation of many.

HOLY WEEK

Palm Sunday, Year A

A Punishment That Brings Us Peace

As we read the Passion account on this day, we know that the love of Jesus is something we can never fully comprehend. When there is a lack of love, then everything is wrong. When love is present it does make things right somehow, sufferingly, agonizingly. In eternity we shall grasp this mystery completely. Love has no Sabbath. Love endures through all things.

The prophet Isaiah speaks these striking words, these wounding words: "Upon him lies a punishment that brings us peace" (Is 53:5, JB). I think punishment and peace are words that we do not often couple. Jesus wanted peace. He was always speaking of peace. But, punishment? Why should he be punished that we should have peace? Is it not because this is the way peace is always wrought?

He wanted peace in his often squabbling, arguing, tedious community. He did bring them peace. In the end he was successful. But he took the punishment for that peace on himself. We are moving swiftly toward the culmination of his punishment on the Cross, his overwhelming love in taking all our sins upon himself. Those supreme hours of punishment stagger the mind and fling the heart down. But during the years when he was training those unlikely candidates for martyrdom who were his community, there was a daily punishment that he was taking on himself. It was not the stark, dramatic punishment of the Cross, but the tedious punishment of always bringing peace, always refusing to be discouraged. He achieved what he achieved—the sanctity, the martyrdom of his own—by taking on himself the punishment. Not just in the Garden when they fell asleep, not just on the Cross, but day in and day out.

It is to this that Jesus is inviting us. His little community lived very closely together. They knew each other very well, or they thought they did. He had to enter into the tedium of everyday to bring the days of glory. This is what he asks of us, we who, to our shame, want things to be made right immediately, that other people change, that other people see, that things go smoothly, without our having to bear the punishment that this requires. What is the punishment? It is the patience, the suffering, the absolute refusal to say, "I have had enough." Never did he say that—ever. We would think he had plenty of reason. We would say that certainly we give him plenty of occasions. But to speak in our poor, halting, human terms, he goes on hoping and hoping; and in the end, if we allow, his hope will be fulfilled. Surely no one but Jesus could ever have envisioned his little community as martyrs. But he did, and he had to go to some length to get his message through to them.

Because Jesus bore the punishment that brought them

the peace in which alone we can love, they did love him in their poor, stumbling way. We cannot love in turmoil. We cannot love when we are fighting against the present reality. But peace comes when we have been willing to take on the punishment of human behavior, beginning with our own, refusing ourselves the dark consolation of despondency, of depression, of saying, "Oh, what's the use?" No one since the beginning of time had such a right to say, "What's the use?" as Jesus did. But he never said it—ever.

We have this great call to holiness, and we are told how to go about it: by loving Jesus, who always bears the punishment of these distasteful human things, these disappointing things. Jesus is always there taking the punishment. We look at you, Jesus, and we love you; then we begin to understand that, to love you, we must be like you. In the day-in, day-out giving, we too give our body, our strength, our effort, our weariness that there may be peace, in which alone love flourishes. We can make so many little warfares within ourselves, within community. But to make peace we look at Jesus and see him patiently bearing the punishment. He did not just tell his own what to do. He showed them what to do by doing it himself.

This is the meaning of community: that we are not warring about who is wrong, but making things right by taking the punishment upon ourselves and, at expense to ourselves, doing what is right. This is to love, and it is as simple as that. To love Jesus is the most demanding thing in life. To love Jesus is the only really rewarding thing in life. Let us determine to be like him and to take upon ourselves the little punishments of human living at close quarters. Then there shall be peace. When there is peace, then love can flourish, and in that love we can be made holy, through Christ our Lord.

Palm Sunday, Year B

Focus

The Apostle says in his Letter to the Philippians that God will give a new form to our lowly body, according to the pattern of Jesus' glorified body (see Phil 3:21). What do we mean by the pattern of his glorified body, which his apostles were to see more than once after the Resurrection? We might think that, after the Resurrection when the body is glorified, there can't be any wounds. But after the Resurrection there was for them, and for all eternity there will be for us, the vision of Jesus' glorified wounds.

How are wounds made glorious? By our deciding what we will do with them. Our Jesus turned his wounds into beauty, and there is not one of us who would say, "Oh, this should not be in eternity." Our poor hearts thrill to the verity that he is always showing his wounds to the Father on our behalf. They are transformed now in glory. Likewise, there is a transformation that we too can make of our own little everyday wounds which sometimes seem so deep and so big and so insufferable to us. How do we transform them into glory? By looking at Jesus, by remembering his suffering which was turned into glory. He accepted suffering and desired it for our sake. And so, in the remembrance of past sufferings, our thoughts should be turned into a glorified memory of them—not a festering memory, but a glorified memory.

Saint Peter Damian says, "Let the serenity of your spirit shine through your face." Let the serenity of our little sufferings, which sometimes seem so large to us because we are so small, shine through our faces. How do we do this? By looking at Jesus, and Jesus alone. We shall be blessed with clear vision, not only of him (as much as we can behold him in this life), but of ourselves.

Saint Gregory of Nyssa says that no trivialities can capture the attention of anyone who has his eyes fixed on Christ. So let us beware of looking away from Christ. Let us ask ourselves some straight questions: What about my own wounds? Do I prefer to look at my wounds, or to offer them to Christ? There are things that should be just between him and me. Do I tend to whine about little things, which seem to be big things to me? Or do I build up my resources each day by looking at Jesus and seeing him alone in what is happening? Nothing can happen without his allowing it. Each day I am either building up my resources or depleting them. Do I sort out my hurts? Do I count them? Do I go over them? Do I sometimes even scratch at them until they are festering? Or does my sometimes wandering gaze quickly return to Christ? Does it return to Christ, or does it return again and again to the memories of past hurts that support the present hurt?

Let us learn this Holy Week to look at the crucifix with more penetration than we have ever looked at it before. Not one of us can fix our gaze on Jesus crucified and say, "What has been asked of me is too much. This hurt is too big. This slight is too humiliating." We cannot do that. We would have to look away from him in order to make that dreadful statement, "This is too much." There are the two alternatives: to look at Jesus crucified and to reflect on Jesus glorified, or to look away, to question. Then we picture not the reality of our own situation so much as what our imagination adds to it to make us resent it.

Now, *looking at* and *seeing* are not the same thing. First we must look and look, but then we must see. There were a lot of people on Calvary, and they were all looking. They were looking at what was happening but they didn't see it, because they made no connection with themselves. When we look at a picture of someone we love very much, we know more and more what the person looks like. We already know what this person looks like, so why do we have the picture? We want to look more and more at the image of someone whom we love, so that looking passes over into seeing. And then in the seeing we are changed as we see that loved image. How much more with the image of our crucified Jesus?

May this coming week deepen this focused gaze. Let us beware of looking away from Christ. It is such a dangerous thing to keep looking at ourselves. Let us pray for one another that we shall be more and more focused on our suffering, all-loving, crucified Jesus and that, looking at the little events of each day which sometimes seem so large to us, we shall come more and more to seeing Jesus alone.

Palm Sunday, Year C

Finding Everything in Him

In the Gospel of the Passion, we are taken to the vision of Christ on the throne of the Cross in his supreme moment of kingship, when humanly he looked least a King and was most *the* King. He was supreme in his choice to redeem us no matter what. No matter that it cost him physical agony, shame (as the world considers shame), the ignominy of seeming the most pitiful failure the world had ever known and seemingly least a King. This was when he was supremely a King; he made his supreme choice that his poor little motley court of creatures was really worth all of this.

Saint Luke gives us a unique glimpse of the dreadful moment when one of the thieves and the bystanders were making fun of him. Then the other thief (and, oh, how grateful we are for him) made much of him. Well-meaning writers comment that the thief said one little thing, "Remember me", and was canonized right away. What the good thief said wasn't a little thing. This was a supreme act of faith in the King because he didn't look like a king, he didn't look like he owned any paradise, he didn't look like he had anything. He didn't have a following anymore, just these women and one man under the Cross. He didn't have anything. The thief made this supreme act of faith to a supreme King. That is why he was canonized. No one else in all the history of time has ever been canonized directly by God: "Truly, I say to you, today you will be with me in Paradise" (Lk 23:43).

The good thief is called "good" because, at the end of his earthly life, as he was being crucified, he repented of his misdeeds and was truthful. He made a great public confession: "Indeed, we have been condemned justly, for the sentence we received corresponds to our crimes" (Lk 23:41, NAB). He didn't say, "I was led into this. My father was a thief before me. I never had a chance." No, he said that he was receiving the just sentence for all his misdeeds. Then he made a tremendous act of faith, enlivened by his public confession. The thief's tremendous act of faith was God's reward for his truthfulness in his public confession; he was enlightened to know that Jesus was innocent. That was all he knew at first; he said, "This man has done nothing wrong." Because he made such a truthful confession of his own great misdeeds, and because of his compassion for an unjustly abused man in a pitiable condition, he was enlightened to make his tremendous act of faith. He was enlightened to see that this was a King; that he would be coming into a kingdom. It must have been like a burst of lightning bolts in his mind—to see suddenly that this man was a King. And so he asks him, "Remember me." He has, so to speak, a right to be remembered, because he remembered to confess his sins and to defend the innocent.

Returning to the terrible phrase, "to make fun of him", we draw back from that in horror. Certainly we don't make fun of Jesus. But we could ask whether we sometimes make little of him. I know what he wants, if I just stop and consider, if I just stop and pray. But when I focus on what *I* want, I make little of what he wants. Let us strive to make more and more of him until we have made everything of him.

Saint Paul says in his Letter to the Colossians, "In him everything continues in being" (Col 1:17, NAB [1989]). If we are immersed in God and find all our meaning in him, and the meaning of everything we do, then we become who we really are. The Apostle goes on to say that "absolute fullness resides in him". If there has ever been an age that was interested in fulfillment, personal fulfillment, ours is the one! This is the watchword of the hour, the day, the week: my personal fulfillment. We can turn that shibboleth of the hour around and say: Yes, I do want my personal fulfillment, that absolute fullness of myself which Scripture says "resides in him". It is striking how often these shibboleths, these watchwords (which are so cheap and shallow), do not know what their ontological meaning could be and really is.

The inspired writer, Paul, also says, "so that primacy may be his in everything". We want to ask ourselves some questions: Does Jesus hold the primacy in every area of my life? Does his humility hold the primacy in my dealings with others, in my work, in my relationships, in my responses? Does his love, which is the essence of himself, hold the primacy in me, or is there something else in me that holds the primacy? Only with the answers to such questions can we grow and continue in being, our real being, which is in him. Then we will have truly entered into the liturgy of this Holy Week.

Monday of Holy Week

He Endured Our Sufferings

It is a wonderful thing that the Church would take one week out of all the year, out of all the days that are holy before God, and say, "This is Holy Week." This is *the* sacred week. But Holy Week does not work, as it were, *"ex opere operato"*. The Church does not say that this is Holy Week, and therefore we automatically become holy in it. No, the Church says this is the great week of opportunity for growing in holiness; this is the week of tremendous graces. But how holy a week it will be for us is ours to decide. We will grow in holiness in this week or not according as we wish, according as we cooperate or do not cooperate with God.

As we look toward the Sacred Triduum, let us consider the words of Isaiah in the Good Friday liturgy, "Yet it was our infirmities that he bore, our sufferings that he endured" (Is 53:4, NAB). What depths of meaning there are in these words! Sometimes we may make the mistake of coming with great fervor to Holy Week, determined to enter into the mystery of the Passion—considered only as the last extreme sufferings of our dear Lord's life. We set these apart with the title "Passion", and yet his whole life was a Passion. *Passio* is "a suffering, an act of patience". As soon as our dear Lord left the womb of his Mother, he began his Passion. What happened in the Garden and on Calvary was the consummation of his lifelong Passion. He suffered as a newborn infant from cold, from an almost complete lack of comfort. As a very small child, he was suffering his Passion of being hunted. Very few children are fugitives in their infancy. He was hunted like a criminal. His life was wanted. As he grew up, he continued in his Passion, always being a Person who was never completely understood by anyone, not even by his Mother. We have the Gospel's word on this, when it says that she didn't understand what he said to her (see Lk 2:50). He continued into young manhood with a deepening of his Passion. He gathered around himself a select group of intimate friends, all of whom, save one, were to desert him; one was to betray him; one was to deny him. This was his Passion.

Interlaced with all these great sufferings were what we might dare to call his little sufferings, which we should love to dwell on. These, too, were part of his Passion, and we do not think nearly enough of them. He took upon himself not only our sorrows, our anguish, our sins, but he took upon himself our weaknesses, our little sorrows. If we look into the happenings of his public life, we will see how much he suffered the very things we suffer. We must not commit the fallacy of thinking he suffered less because he was perfect. Just as a member of our bodies which is more sensitive suffers more, he suffered more, not less, because his sensibilities were absolutely perfect, because he was, even humanly speaking, the most refined Person who ever lived. More than any other person who has ever lived, he suffered from boorishness, coarseness, uncouthness. Because his was so perfect an intellect, he suffered more than anyone else from others' dullness, lack of understanding, stupidity. Occasionally he lifted a curtain from his interior life and let us see, surely for our comfort, his very human reactions to things. He said to his disciples, with whom he bore so patiently over and over again, "How long am I to be with you?" (Mt 17:17). He let show his sense of frustration with these people, dull as we are dull.

We should look into our own lives and relate our little unspectacular sufferings to the Passion of Christ. He has taken upon himself not only our sins but our infirmities, our weaknesses, and he has taken them upon himself fully. He understands them. Have you ever thought that at times he must have been extremely bored with people, and that this was part of his Passion, this was part of his suffering? Certainly he did not find the conversation of his apostles scintillating and enchanting. It must have been a great trial to his human nature. Do we think often enough of the sense of disappointment that he suffered? This is a thing that we have all experienced. We can be disappointed with events, disappointed with one another, and we become very disappointed with ourselves. Our dear Lord could never experience disappointment with himself, yet surely no one ever experienced it with events and with people as he did. People were always disappointing him. People were always failing to come up to the standards he would have liked them to reach. This was part of his Passion.

We have a duty to relate our little disappointments to the sufferings of his Passion. We shall never sweat blood. We shall never be nailed to a cross. It is very unlikely that anyone would ever spit in our face. It is extremely difficult to imagine that anyone would ever strike us on our cheek. We shall not have to carry a cross and fall under it; we shall not have nails through our hands. But we shall always have many little things to suffer. We must not allow ourselves to forget that he knows them all. He took them upon himself. He didn't just endure them as something that human nature could not escape. He wanted to experience them.

Tuesday of Holy Week

He Endured Our Sufferings (continued)

Jesus took our weaknesses upon himself and he carried them as a man carries a burden he is glad to carry. In the Garden when our dear Lord suffered his agony, he confronted evil as no one else ever could. Only God could do this. He stood, as it were, face to face with all the sin of all the people who had ever been or ever would be. He confronted this stench, this mess. He confronted it, and it flung him to the ground, and it caused blood instead of sweat to press out through his pores. He confronted it in truth, and he recognized it. Into this terrible confrontation were gathered all the little sufferings of his life —all the little human futilities he had experienced. The human frustrations, the human disappointments seemed to come to a fine point in this confrontation with evil in the Garden. We can suffer a great deal if we can see clearly the good that is going to come out of it. We can make great sacrifices if the goal is sure. In the Garden during this terrible confrontation with evil, with malice, with sin, our dear Lord knew that what he was about to suffer would be futile for many people, that it would be unavailing for their salvation, that even the blood of

God poured out on the Cross would prove unavailing for the salvation of many who would refuse the fruits of the redemption. No one ever suffered a sense of futility, a temptation to frustration, to utter disappointment as he did; he grappled with it and he overcame it and he entered then into the last stage of his Passion.

Let us examine two implications of this: truth with ourselves and love for one another. On an infinitely lower plane we must confront the evil in ourselves, and this is what I mean by truth. There is a mass of imperfection within our soul, and we must confront this; we must face it with truth. God has said, "I am the truth." Therefore when we offend truth, we render direct offense to God. How do we offend against truth? Do we tell lies? Of course not. But sometimes we are very untruthful to ourselves. We will not confront the evil in ourselves. We will not confront the imperfection in ourselves. How then can we enter into the mystery of his Passion? How can we hope to be forgiven for what we will not admit? How can we be sorry for our imperfections if we do not acknowledge our imperfections? This is what lies at the heart of the mystery that so many saints have urged upon our attention: that our faults do not hinder our union with God if they are admitted, if they are repented of, if we firmly resolve with God's grace to overcome them. What does tragically hinder our union with God, what makes it impossible, is that we would not love the truth, that we would not acknowledge our imperfections, and worst of all that we would try to pretend that our imperfections are virtues. We cannot be sorry for what we do not admit. If we are not sorry, then we cannot be forgiven. So let us think deeply on this: that we have our own little Garden of Gethsemane where we must confront the evil of imperfection in ourselves, wrestle with it in acknowledging the truth of this mess that is within us, and then reach out humbly for God's grace. His grace will come like the comforting angel, if we love the truth.

If we love the truth about ourselves and admit it, we are growing in humility. If we love the truth and are growing in humility, then at the same time we are growing in love for one another. Let us never allow ourselves to forget that we shall never compassionate Christ more than we compassionate one another. No one shall ever love God in greater measure than she loves her companions.

Mercy is not a cool, casual idea of forgiveness. It is not a condescending "looking down" upon these imperfect companions of ours and agreeing that we shall put up with these things. This already indicates that we have placed ourselves on a higher plane and we simply "put up" with these other people. This is not compassion, *com-pati*, "to suffer with". Compassion is to take the person as she is into the embrace of our love and our spirit. It is to enter into her imperfections and her sufferings. This is what mercy really is. If we do not have this kind of love for one another, we cannot have compassion for our Divine Spouse in his sufferings.

Jesus is saying to us at this sacred ending of Lent that now above all is the acceptable time, acceptable as never before. We shall make it an operative Holy Week in our own lives by a confrontation of truth, by our own Gethsemane, by our own struggle with ourselves. We shall enter into compassion with him in exactly the same measure that we compassionate one another. This is the greatest incentive to charity for one another that we could have. We have all experienced that when one who is dear to us suffers, our first reflex emotion is, "Oh, if only I could bear this in her place!" This is the way we should enter into Holy Week. "Oh, if only we could suffer it for him." The agony and the crucifixion and the Resurrection took place at precise moments in history, but they are also in God's mind, where there is no past nor future; there is only the everlasting present. All our sins were present in the Garden.

Jesus saw our infirmities, our weaknesses, our little sufferings of futility, depression, frustration, lack of understanding from others and our own misunderstandings of others, and he said, as it were, "Oh, if only I could take them on myself." And he did. He took them and he carried them. We should give those words back to him and say to him with our love and with our truth, "Oh, if only we could suffer it for you." If we do, he will allow us to enter into the mystery of the Passion. There is only one way for us to enter into the Passion, and that is by way of compassion. This is the way the Mother of God herself entered into the Passion. She is the Queen of compassion. She is compassionate toward us. She compassionated him. She will teach us, she will lead us, because she is the Mother of sorrows and the Mother of Joys—the Mother of life. Each of our lives is meant to reproduce the Passion of Christ not by bloody sweats, not by nails, but by suffering in these little unspectacular, unglamorous ways. This is our passion, and it is only through this passion and this cross that we shall be brought to the glory of his Resurrection.

Wednesday of Holy Week

Assent to Glory

What do we mean by glorifying God? We know that *to glorify* means "to exalt, to make radiant, to make to shine forth". We look to the Scriptures, and one of the references to God being glorified that we find in Saint John's Gospel is indeed startling: the incident of Judas. Our Lord knew that this disciple whom he himself had called, about whose vocation there was no possible doubt, was planning to betray him. With divine consciousness he knew that this was part of the divine plan of redemption. As a man, he still made one last invitation of tenderness. He dipped the morsel of bread into the sauce and handed it to him with those blessed fingers as a last chance, a sign of intimate friendship, a sign of esteem (see Jn 13:26). And it didn't work. He could not reach his heart. So he said to him, "What you are going to do, do quickly,"— as if to say, "Go and do it. I can do no more."

The apostles were very confused about what Judas was doing. They thought he was going out to get some provisions, or that perhaps our dear Lord was sending him on some mission for the poor. But then Jesus said, "Now is the Son of man glorified." We can well suppose these were the words they had been waiting to hear, because they thought they knew what it meant to be glorified. Can we not see them reacting to this? Now it was going to happen. Their minds were buzzing with thrones and power and the anticipation of reigning with him.

Earlier in John's Gospel, when some Greeks asked to see Jesus, he responded, "The hour has come for the Son of man to be glorified" (Jn 12:23). The apostles must certainly have been surprised at the words that immediately followed. "Truly, truly, I say to you, unless a grain of wheat falls into the earth and dies, it remains alone; but if it dies, it bears much fruit" (Jn 12:24). Instead of talking about thrones and exaltation and obeisance and victory and triumph and worldly prestige, he said that glory —God's glory and his own glory—has something to do with dying. But always, in his many references to sacrifice, to abnegation, to dying, he is saying something very positive. It is not just that the grain of wheat falls into the earth and dies, and that's it. But this is for a purpose. Death is never its own end. Death is always a preface, a prelude, an avenue toward something better.

The apostles should have remembered those words at the terrible moment when Jesus revealed that one of their own was about to betray him. After his last attempt to rescue Judas from himself had failed, Jesus said to them, "Now is the Son of man glorified" (Jn 13:31), a very mysterious word revealing to us how God is glorified. Our dear Lord had assented in his heart to the full plan of divine redemption, of which this betrayal was a part.

There was no human suffering that he would not experience. Caught up in exaltation of spirit, he had given the assent of his heart to the divine plan of redemption, and God had been glorified.

While there is a great sadness in considering this, there is also a marvelous expansion of thought and of spirit, and a great incentive to us. God is glorified by every assent of the heart to whatever suffering God has planned as our part in the redemption of the world. Think of that. Always, when the heart assents to whatever sacrifice God asks, a larger picture opens out before us. The more God is glorified by the assent of the heart, the more do we see how God is asking us to glorify him further. This means that we die to self-involvement, to entanglements, to what would make us remain alone with self, involved with self, entangled with self—a terrible state to be in. We want to lead lives of much dying so that much fruit can spring up. This is what it is to glorify God.

Our Lord says something that shakes our human hearts, showing us how fully a man is this Savior of ours. His heart, incapable of sin, was subject to human turmoil. We must not think we do him honor by pretending that it was not. He was perhaps tempted to rest in his sorrow at ingratitude, to rest in his disappointment. He is opening his human heart in confidence to us, as he opened it so many times in the Scriptures, when he says, "Now is my soul troubled. And what shall I say? 'Father, save me from this hour'? No, for this purpose I have come to this hour" (Jn 12:27). It is so touching what he reveals of himself to us. He ends with the same word with which he began, as though he lifted up that beautiful head of his and said, "Father, glorify your name."

We are not engaging in any kind of fantasy when we picture this scene to ourselves and see what our dear Lord's expression must have been. Can we not imagine those beautiful eyes filling with tears when he says, "Save me from this hour"? He was a man of his own race, and he had his own human temperament. The Scriptures tell us that he sobbed out loud over Jerusalem. He cried for Lazarus. We see that noble head lifting as he says, "No, for this purpose I have come to this hour" and then his eyes lifting to heaven as he says, "Father, glorify your name."

God is glorified by our victory over our own human turmoil and tossings. It is not that we go serenely through life untroubled by temptation and unafraid, not subject to the vacillations of the human heart; but it is out of struggle and temptation that we turn to God and say, "But it is for this reason that I dwell within this family or community." This is marvelous holy living: many assents of the heart, much dying to self, much burying in the ground so that much fruit may spring forth to glorify the Father.

Jesus tells us that it is to the glory of his Father that we should bring forth much fruit. Perhaps the Father is most glorified by the most hidden fruit. Saint Paul tells us that our battles are with principalities and powers. Well, obviously this means struggles of the heart, struggles with pride, struggles with vanity, all of these struggles with the things that belong to the fallen angels—pride, disobedience, *non serviam*: "I won't do it." The Father adds to his glory by our bearing much fruit in these battles. Every secret victory of the heart glorifies God throughout his Holy Church.

Then, like a master teacher, Jesus draws together these great thoughts that he had given them, these great revelations that the apostles probably understood very dimly, and that we also understand dimly. We must penetrate them again and again so that, like the apostles, we can come, through our own living of them, to understand them better. He says, "A servant is not greater than his master" (Jn 13:16). We must decline to have a false goal of wishing to arrive at a point where there is no struggle, what one would call a languid "holiness". Of course, there is no such thing. "This is the way I glorify my Father, and this is the way you will glorify my Father." There is no other way. No disciple is greater than his Master.

There is a cyclic movement in glorification. We never glorify God without God glorifying us. We never allow God's radiance to shine forth without him making us radiant beyond what we could have dreamed. And so he says, "Now is the Son of man glorified, and in him God is glorified" (Jn 13:31). Then, "If God is glorified in him, God will also glorify him in himself, and he will glorify him at once" (Jn 13:32). It is doubtful whether the apostles understood this at the moment, but they grew in understanding. Later in life they experienced in themselves that whenever the heart gives assent to God's dear will, that whenever the grain of wheat falls into the ground and dies, much fruit is brought forth. Whenever the heart, by God's grace in the soul, emerges out of turmoil into God's victory and God is glorified, the person, too, is glorified. One has new strength to give new assents, and one also has a new understanding of the great fruit that comes out of dying, experiencing in one's own self what it is to come into the radiance of God out of the dark turmoil of human weakness. And so the person is glorified. There is a new strength, a new understanding.

We can never make any effort for God without God immediately sending it to redound upon ourselves. We cannot glorify God without immediately being glorified ourselves. Our dear Lord says, "I glorified you on earth . . . Now, Father, glorify me in your own presence with the glory which I had with you before the world was made" (Jn 17:4, 5). We are made radiant every time we allow the radiance of God to shine forth. We are made strong every time we use his grace to triumph over human weakness. God will not accept our glorifying him without glorifying us.

Holy Thursday

Lord, Let Your Love Come Upon Us

We come together in one of the Church's most solemn hours, an hour in which one may dare to say the Church is most herself. She is reenacting, reviewing, and asking of herself what she should be. The Church, the Bride of such a Master, goes looking for her Bridegroom on this day. She finds him, not seated in glory, but at the feet of his own. This, too, is where we find him, abased beyond measure in the Blessed Sacrament. The Church finds her Master lowly, merciful, forgiving, hoping on and on that the message of his love, his humility, his mercy, and his hope in his own, will yet be fulfilled in us.

For this particular day, our dear Lord put into my heart a very daring prayer we pray often in the great Psalm 119 (Grail, v. 41): "O Lord, let your love come upon us." This is not a matter of something sweet and comforting coming upon us. What is his love that we pray may come upon us? It is an all-demanding thing. Speaking in our human, stumbling words, when the love of the Father came upon the Son in the Incarnation, that love, that desire that men be saved, brought the incarnate Son to crucifixion, to desolation, to all manner of suffering, beyond what we can ever suffer or even comprehend. For the love of Jesus to come upon us means that we are prepared to suffer all things, without lingering in disappointment, without setting up a tent for ourselves in discouragement, but willing to suffer on and on. It is to become, in God's light, invincible in suffering. This is what it means for the love of the Lord to come upon us.

When the love of the Lord came in its fullness upon the apostles at Pentecost, it swept away all of those petty ambitions and faultfindings with one another—each one finding fault with the others so that he himself might look better, pushing the others back so that he himself might come forward. But the love of the Lord came upon them and all of these petty ambitions were swept up into the fulfillment of an ambition which even they would never have dreamed of: that they would be martyrs, that they would be found worthy to die for him. Previously, they would not have seen this as a prize. They thought of glory, of thrones, of serenity, of being untroubled, of reigning, of lording it over others, but never had they ambitioned themselves as martyrs. But the love of the Lord came upon them and this is what happened.

Saint Paul tells us what happens when the love of the Lord comes upon us. He describes its effects on ourselves and on others: "Love is patient and kind; love is not quick-tempered, it does not brood over injury" (1 Cor 13:4, 5). And, "Love endures all things." This is what it means to have the love of Jesus come upon us. So let us be careful of this dangerous prayer. Let us be sure that we know what we are asking for, and let us ask to have that love come upon us so that we may be like him.

Jesus saw pride in his apostles, along with a lack of realism, an unwillingness to confront their own pettiness and their own errors and mistakes. What did he do about it? He humbled himself. He made up in himself what was wanting in his own. He chose a setting that undoubtedly we would never have chosen for the greatest of all miracles, his coming to abide forever among us in the Eucharist. He chose the greatest feast in the liturgy of the Old Testament, and it was carried out by his own poor apostles with bickering. But we see Jesus never yielding to the full measure of human discouragement. We might have said, "Nothing can be done with these people—at such a time, to be acting in this fashion!" Anyone else would have arrived at the ultimate discouragement. Everyone but Jesus, who went down on his knees before his own obtuse, argumentative, proud apostles, and washed their feet.

Then he told them, and us, that there is a sign by which all the world can know who belongs to him. He did not talk about miracle-working, about herculean feats of body or spirit. He spoke of love. He prayed that the love of the Father, which had come upon him in his humanity and made it impossible for him to give up on his own, would come upon us. He spoke not of the marvelous homilies that the apostles were to give when the Holy Spirit would come upon them, nor of their power to raise the dead to life, but the sign he gave was that they should love one another. Never can we ponder this enough. He didn't even say, "By this everyone will know you are mine, that you make such protestations of love of me", but "that you love one another".

This is what it means for the love of God to come upon us. This is the measure, this is the one and only infallible sign. On this day we see the Lord of heaven and earth on the ground, on his knees before his own, in whom we recognize our own dullness, our own limitedness, our own shamefulness, our own pettiness, our own drabness. It's all there. He counted this as an appropriate setting in which to give us his Body and his Blood, his Soul and his Divinity to remain with us forever. Surely our small minds would say it was the wrong place, the wrong hour, the wrong people. But Jesus thought otherwise. From these, his own disciples, eventually to be ennobled by his own love and his own humility and his own indefatigable hope in them, came the Church—the Church enduring two thousand years and more, the Church enduring yet in us, gathered here in our little upper room. The love of the Father come upon Jesus did all of this.

We are most his when we show that his love has come upon us, when in our dealings with one another we are at the feet of one another, always forgiving, always hoping, always determined to abstain from the luxury of discouragement about others or about ourselves—for if Jesus has believed in each one of us, we must believe, not in ourselves, but in his belief in us. In this we can believe.

Let us be renewed on this day. He said to them, "What I am doing you do not know now, but afterward you will understand" (Jn 13:7). The fullness of time has come at Pentecost, in the revelation of God through his Church, and we have the means and the grace to understand that this is the triumph of God: unflagging humility in those who belong to him, so that it approaches a little more the humility of the God-Man. This is the triumph of the Church. This is the vindication of God's hope that we grow in love. So let us pray for one another, that the love of God which makes all things possible may come upon us. This is the only description of a successful community: that we love one another, each of us, all of us, no matter what—as Jesus loved his community, no matter what, and sought to the very end to save them.

Good Friday

❧

We Have No King but Jesus

I find it very helpful in Holy Week to take some words in the Gospel narratives that tear at the heart, and to turn them the other way. "They were plotting against him to catch him in something he might say" (see Lk 11:54). Yes, we are trying to catch him in something he might say, too. We don't want to miss a word. We want to catch it all. "They were watching him closely" (see Lk 14:1). Yes, we want to watch him all the time. We don't ever want to take our eyes off him. Scripture says that Judas looked for an opportunity to betray Jesus; we want to turn that around and look for an opportunity to be faithful to him. When the crowd cries, "We have no king but Caesar" (Jn 19:15), we cry out instead, "We have no King but Jesus." Let us turn all of those terrible things into acts of love.

We want it to be said of us as it was of Peter, "You were with Jesus the Nazorean . . . even your speech gives you away" (see Mt 26:71, 73). Our speech, our manner should show that we have been with Jesus. We know that those who are together often begin even to talk in the same way, with the same accent. Everyone should notice that we talk like Jesus.

When, in his driving desire for self-preservation, Peter said, "I do not know the man" (Mt 26:72), he spoke better than he realized at the time. This denial came out of his cowardice, and we are all cowards along with him. But there was a deeper truth that Peter must have understood better later on. No, he didn't really know Jesus. Peter didn't yet know the depth of Jesus' mercy, that he would be so ready to forgive, even when, in his hour of greatest need, the head of his community failed him. Later Peter would come to know Jesus truly in the depth of his mercy, forgiveness, and love.

Then we read of Judas' betrayal, that he "deeply regretted what he had done" (Mt 27:3, NAB). But he didn't regret it deeply enough. Now surely on this day we look back, as we have been looking back all of Lent; and we see the dreadful things we do, the small things that we do, our failures to rise to the opportunities to love and to grow and to be holy. We regret them, but do we regret them enough? Is our regret merely an emotion? Or does it include the will to change? Peter had a great emotional regret. He went out and wept bitterly, and surely he must have wept a long time. Tradition says he wept for the rest of his life and thought it too short a time to weep for having failed the One who loved him so much, who had never failed him. But his regret had to be more than tears; it had to lead to the will to change. At the end of Saint Peter's mortal life we see he had indeed changed. He who always knew just what should be done, who could correct the Master if he wasn't running things right, who was so proud, so ambitious, would not allow his executioners to crucify him in the same position as Jesus. As we picture him there on the cross, upside down, knowing himself not worthy to die in the same position as his Lord, we see someone who really regretted deeply what he had done and had willed to change. He had let love truly overpower him.

In the Book of Revelation Saint John says, "Every eye will see him, every one who pierced him" (Rev 1:7). Truly this is a heart-shaking word, speaking of Christ coming in the full glory of his kingship at the end of time. We shall see what we have done. Saint John says, "All the peoples of the earth will lament him." Surely the heart wants to weep. We shall lament the vision of what we have done, where we have failed, where we have wounded the King. But we can reduce the lamentation by the healing that we bring now, healing to the wounds of the King. How is he wounded by us? How is he wounded in the kingdom of the Church in so many ways, which we are called to heal? Each one must answer that for herself. We will have less cause for bitter lamenting on the day of glory, the day of Judgment, in the measure in which we have made reparation upon earth.

Holy Saturday

The Sword of Sorrow

Standing beneath the Cross, the Mother of Jesus experienced the fulfillment of the prophecy spoken by Simeon on that long-ago day when she brought her infant Son to the Temple. Truly on Calvary a sword of sorrow did pierce her soul, that the thoughts of many hearts might be revealed (see Lk 2:35). There is no true love without suffering. It is an indispensable ingredient of love. Nothing great is ever accomplished for God without suffering. If the most pure soul of Mary needed to be pierced that God's purpose in many hearts should be revealed, shall we not think it necessary that our souls be pierced? Shall we think that we can spread the Kingdom of God's love upon earth without swords in our souls? This is not inconsistent with joy. When we love, we are glad to suffer. The soul should be pierced in order that others may grow in love and that we may grow in love. In fact, the more we love, the greater is our capacity to suffer. The greater our willingness to suffer, the greater is our power to love.

Let the soul be pierced with the sword of willing suffering, that out of many other hearts, thoughts may be revealed. We shall learn only in eternity about the closed hearts, out of which God's thought was not being revealed or to whom God's thought could not be revealed, and which were opened through our poor instrumentality when we allowed our souls to be pierced with swords of suffering, as our Lady did. Our hearts and souls are to be rent, not kept for ourselves, not kept shut, not kept safe, but wounded, made more and more vulnerable, that faith may flow out on a dark world, that love may flow out on a starved world. May this be so.

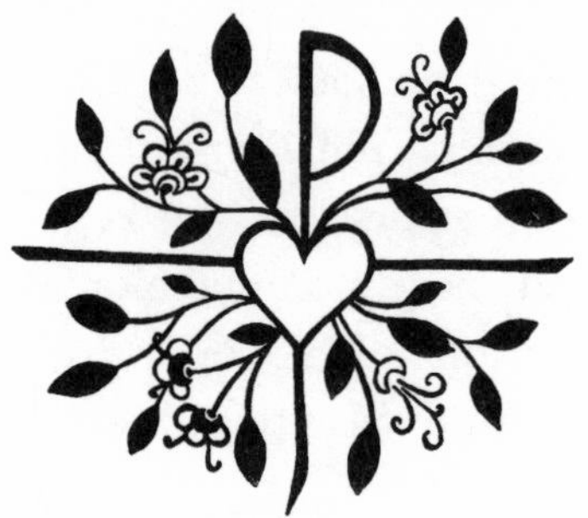

The Resurrection

It is surely not hard to see the joy of our Lady in the Resurrection. The Scriptures say nothing about Jesus appearing to her. According to the evangelists, he appeared to Mary Magdalen, then he appeared to the apostles. In my college religion class, the priest who was our professor said, "Well, you really don't think the Scriptures have to mention that? Some things the Scriptures can take for granted." He said it in a tone of voice implying, "Any fool knows to whom he appeared first." Our Lady had the joy that she had never wavered in her belief, that in all of these terrible things throughout his Passion and death her faith never wavered. When everything was going wrong, everything was failure, and everything was horror, she never stopped believing. Imagine the crown of Joy at the Resurrection for her who had never stopped believing.

APPENDIX

The Stations of the Cross

I. Jesus Is Condemned to Die

The Word of God
Condemned to die
Has no word to say.

Silence is speech of innocence.
Guilt with words brims over.

Unbrim my sinful heart,
Jesu,
Of words.

II. Jesus Takes Up His Cross

Take it up?
No, put it down.
Show them who's king here!

Power's the thing. So, cast away
Impediment to glory.

Cross-lore is gained alone
By lift-
ing it.

III. Jesus Falls, the First Time

One must, of course,
Look up to God
On his lofty height.

Stature is sign of high command.
Who is this, felled and fallen?

Who will look down on God,
And stand
Again?

IV. Jesus Meets His Mother

Nothing to do,
But only be
In useless agony?

Where is the point of standing by
With nothing to do save be?

Mother, my busy soul
Come teach
To be.

V. Simon Helps Jesus Carry His Cross

Teeth of the ego
Gnash at help
Given grudgingly.

"So, never mind. I have no need
Of drafted aid from you."

Bend down my haughty head,
Lord, rip
My sails.

VI. Veronica Wipes the Face of Jesus

You do not look
Much like a God
Framed to hang on dreams.

Are You there, under sweat and blood
Uglied with dust of falls?

And can my love be
Towel to
Show truth?

VII. Jesus Falls, the Second Time

How does one face
The face not seen
Except by face of earth?

Why's not a cloud His vehicle
To speed Him from our sight?

Where shall we dare find faith
To lift
God up?

VIII. The Weeping Daughters of Jerusalem

Please do not say
We should not weep.
Tears are all we have.

Must we go spend them on ourselves?
Here's our woman's gift:

Some tears, some stubborn hope
In help-
less love.

IX. Jesus Falls, the Third Time

So comes the end,
No arabesque,
Just sprawl of last defeat

With all grace gone
And all strength drained.

All's over now. But God
Got up
Again.

X. Jesus Is Stripped of His Garments

All the excuses
Tailor-made
To robe my nakedness

Of sin and fault and misery
Come un-seamed, Jesu, here.

How shall I cry: "Too hard!"
Lord, af-
ter this?

XI. Jesus Is Nailed to the Cross

No climbing now
Up Thabor's height,
No boat on Galilee,

Only You roam creation free.
Tell me what's victory:

You found a place to lay
Your head
At last.

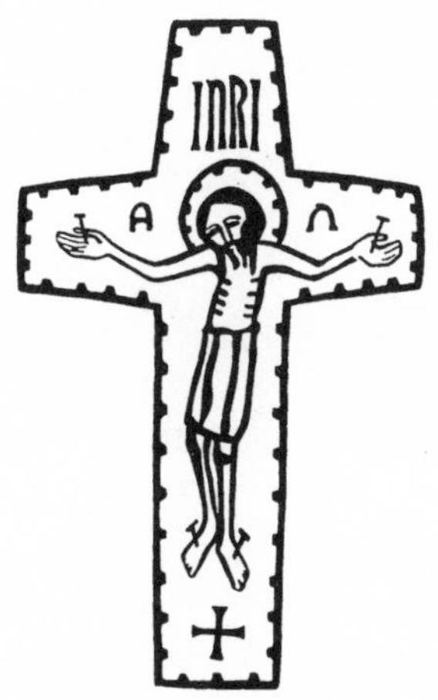

XII. Jesus Dies on the Cross

Yours only, Lord
To own this word:
"It is consummated."

Too swiftly soon I cry: "The end!"
But this word I may claim:

"Father, forgive them,"
I can say,
"and me."

XIII. Jesus Is Laid in His Mother's Arms

There's lap of love
For all dead dreams
That yet may rise again.

In your arms, Mary,
Hold them fast

Against all signs,
For resurrection's
Hour.

XIV. Jesus Is Placed in the Sepulchre

Sleeping, You sleep
In sepulchre
Sealed with finality.

Restless in death,
I twist and cry

Until You break my heart
To set
Me free.

First published in Mother Mary Francis, *Summon Spirit's Cry*, 60–65.

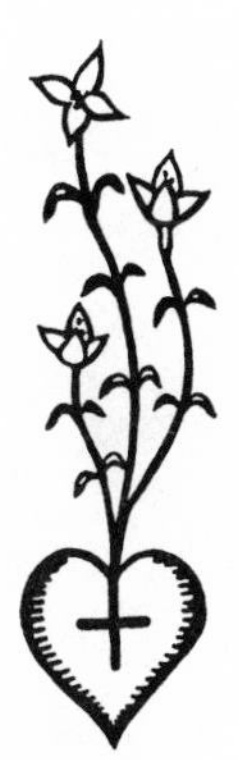